"An easy-to-understand treatise of how to make money whether you are 18 or 80!"

—Doug McKim

"A logically organized, sensibly written, plain-English guide for the average investor. I'm now set up to profit furiously."

—John Sinclair

"I found Hicks and Hiebert's innovative money management tips instantly rewarding."

—Jeff Craig

"The concept of having it all, money now and security later, is most appealing—and I want it all. The authors deliver with style and make the subject fun. Making Money the Old-Fashioned Way expanded my financial awareness."

—Gail B. Brown

"Armed with this book, my husband and I were finally motivated to see a tax advisor. Purchasing Making Money the Old-Fashioned Way may have been the smartest financial move we've ever made. It's a hit! Four stars out of four!"

—Maralyn Ryan

"Prize winning broker and prize winning writer. Ron's common sense approach to money so appealed to me that I shared this book with my clients all of whom praised its style and content."

—Jackie Charlesworth

"You took the mystery out of personal finance for me! Now I have a clear plan that's really working for me! Thanks for making your book so practical and easy to understand!"

—Penny Darnell

"This could profitably be read by every grade twelve graduate. In fact it might be considered required reading for them. A lifetime of bad monetary habits might be stanched at the very outset."

—DFK Dawson

Making Money

The Old-Fashioned Way

RON HIEBERT
GRAHAM HICKS

ARNOLD
PUBLISHING LTD.

Arnold Publishing Ltd.
Suite 101, 10301–104 Street
Edmonton, Alberta, Canada, T5J 1B9
TEL: (403) 426-2998
1-800-563-2665
FAX: (403) 426-4607

Authors: Ron Hiebert and Graham Hicks

Canadian Cataloguing in Publication Data
Hiebert, Ron, 1953-
    Making money the old-fashioned way

    ISBN 0-919913-11-3
    1. Finance, Personal. 2. Investments.
I. Hicks, Graham, 1950-   II. Title.
HG179.H53 1993   332.024   093-091110-5

Project Team
Project Director: Phyllis A. Arnold
Copy Editor: Barbara Demers
Design: Jill Murrin
Illustrations: Peter Bishop
Charts: Linda Bondarevich (Turner Word Services)
Index: Kathy Garnsworthy
Production: James Grose, Linda Henschell, Jill Murrin,
    Corinna Kennedy Lee

Manufacturer: The Jasper Printing Group Ltd.

Printed and bound in Canada

Table of Contents

While the scenarios described in this book are realistic, all characters described are fictional, and are not intended to refer to any individuals past or present.

The Authors

Ron Hiebert has been an investment advisor with the investment firm Scotia McLeod since 1983. In 1991, he won the investment community's Distinction Award for the province of Alberta. Hiebert received his Master's of Science in administration from California State University, Los Angeles, and his Bachelor of Arts at Ambassador College, Pasadena, California. A popular radio financial commentator, Hiebert is married with four children. He resides in Edmonton, Alberta.

Graham Hicks is an editor and columnist with the Edmonton *Sun* newspaper. His undergraduate studies were at the University of Toronto, and he has worked at the Ottawa *Citizen*, Brandon *Sun*, and *Edmonton Journal* before joining the Edmonton *Sun* in 1981. Hicks is married with two children. He lives in Edmonton.

This book is dedicated to our most patient wives, Linda Hiebert and Maria Hicks.

Introduction

I've been rich and I've been poor. Rich is better.

—Sophie Tucker

This book may surprise you. It's so simple.

It's so simple to make a life-long financial plan. Following a plan of making and saving money the old-fashioned way can allow you to be reasonably financially independent after working 20 to 30 years.

Look at Jeremy Stuart, Jim Melnyk, or Joyce Richards. Stuart is only 26, still a student, and he's well on his way to financial independence. Melnyk was a salaried employee with a car dealership. He's not working anymore, and he's living on $57 000 a year. Richards, long retired as a school teacher, still enjoys managing investments worth over $500 000.

There's no magic, no quick buck, no speculation. We're writing this book for the average person, the Jims and Joyces of this world; for those who didn't make a killing on the stock market, or become millionaires because of a lucky land deal. We're writing this book for the typical man or woman— salaried, married, a couple of kids: For those whose immediate dream is to kiss the mortgage goodbye, save for retirement, and, along the way, afford a couple of recreational toys.

The old-fashioned way of making money doesn't take a Ph.D., a Master's degree, or even a high school degree.

Ask Lily Wong. She didn't even go to elementary school. Lily had everything going against her. She came to Canada penniless, and had to struggle with a foreign language. When her husband died, she was left with eight young mouths to feed. She spent her entire working life behind the counter of the family's corner grocery store. Mrs. Wong got quite a shock recently. Revenue Canada decided she owed the government $225 000 in back taxes. She didn't know tax had to be paid on the interest earned from Canada Savings Bonds. All she ever invested in, besides her store, were Canada Savings Bonds. She's 92. Her savings bonds alone are worth over $900 000. Even paying the back taxes owing leaves Mrs. Wong with complete financial security.

This book is about becoming a Lily Wong, a Jim Melnyk, a

Joyce Richards, or a Jeremy Stuart. It's about achieving financial security.

Contrary to credit-card mentality—spend now, pay later—building a financial nest-egg hasn't changed much over the years. If you work as hard as your parents and grandparents, drive second-hand cars, pay off the mortgage, and invest your savings carefully, then you can realistically plan to spend the last third of your life in comfort … without being forced to work. If you start at 20, then you could retire a little earlier. If you are starting to organize your finances at 50, then you need to work quickly. But it's never too late, and some retirement income is much better than none at all.

Like most of us, you probably dream about the day you can say "so long" to the boss. You dream about escaping to Hawaii—every year—when it's -40 ℃ back home. You hope to enjoy retirement without any financial worries. Still, unless you plan on being a hermit, retirement takes money. This book will show you how to get it.

Looking in the Mirror

It is a test of values, of what things we will give up in order to make other things secure.

—Bernard Baruch

To be successful at accumulating wealth, you *must* set up a financial plan. It's not a big complicated project. Thinking about it is far harder than actually doing it. All you need is paper, a pen, and two hours of your time.

What you're creating is a financial road map. Like any good navigator, you have to know where you are now and where you want to go. Then you can plan on how to get there.

Taking Stock

Start by adding up your "assets": the cash value of everything you own. This isn't a deliberately optimistic or pessimistic

statement. It's not being prepared for your estranged spouse's lawyer, or for income tax purposes.

What you own includes cash in the bank, investments, real estate, registered retirement savings plans, and your personal belongings. List them on one side of your piece of paper, estimate each item's value, and then add up the total.

On the depressing side of this ledger, write down all your liabilities: the people and institutions you owe money to—mortgages, bank loans, credit cards. Add them up. Subtract your liabilities from your assets, and, vóila! your NET WORTH.

Where you are now sets the course for your financial activities in the years to come.

If you're broke and under 40, don't worry. You've got lots of time to correct the problem. If you're past the big Four-Oh and find you're not worth much, you'll have to do more than buy lottery tickets to achieve financial freedom.

No Pain, No Gain

Budgeting is tough.

Being broke is even tougher. Budgeting is simply taking control of your finances. Nothing more and nothing less.

Paying off your debts and saving money is less stressful than spending the rest of your life with your back against a financial wall.

A budget does not take hours to figure out every month. Nor does it mean living like a monk. It simply means sticking to a spending and savings plan that will leave you well off when you choose to retire.

Budgeting Nuts and Bolts

Budgeting is very simple.

Take another piece of paper. Draw a line down the centre. On the left side, list how much you earn every month. On the right side, list how much you spend every month.

If your expenses are higher than your income, then cut back your expenses. Or increase your income. That's it.

Once your income is higher than your expenses, what's left is for saving and investing.

You *must* build an emergency stash of cash before starting an investment program. You should have three months' worth of take-home pay put aside in a form you can easily use—like a savings bond or a savings account. Unless you have an emergency fund, it's too easy to ruin your budget when a financial crisis arrives.

Why Budgets Fail

Being too austere: If you deny yourself all of life's pleasures, budgeting becomes too tough, and you set yourself up for failure.

Being unrealistic: Room has to be left in a budget for the unexpected. Nobody can exactly tell what their future expenses will be. By estimating expenses on the high side, chances are you'll be pleasantly surprised when you come in under budget.

Not having an emergency fund: Financial crises kill budgets. An emergency fund keeps budgets alive.

Spending too much time on your budget: After a while, budgeting has to become intuitive. Tracking every little expenditure just takes too much time.

How to Save

If you're not forced to save, you probably won't.

Unless you have a car payment, a mortgage payment, or a deduction off your pay cheque, it's hard not to be a spineless jelly fish when it comes to putting money aside.

Be smart: recognize your human failings and install a forced savings plan.

If you have a mortgage, then look at accelerated pay-downs of that mortgage. Every dollar you commit beyond your normal payments is a forced saving.

Most employers offer *forced* savings plans. Payroll deductions towards a Canada Savings Bond is an obvious compulsory saving plan. A $41.66 deduction twice a month will give you a $1000 savings bond at the end of a year.

Many companies offer employee stock purchase plans via payroll deductions. Stock purchase is an excellent investment, if you believe in your company's future. Employees are sometimes able to purchase stock at less than market price.

Your surest road to short-term savings is to set up, at your bank, trust company, or credit union, an automatic transfer of part of your paycheque into a savings account. As long as you resist the impulse to dip into that savings account, you should be able to build up enough cash to invest in longer-term, higher-yielding investments.

Rule of 72

The time has come to talk about the magic of compound interest. "Compounded" interest is what will earn you financial freedom.

Interest is the money your money earns as a "rental fee" for lending it to somebody else. If you again lend out that "rental fee," you begin to earn interest on the interest. As you do this over and over again, you "compound" your investment.

This simple illustration points out the power of compounding. It's called the "rule of 72."

Take the number 72 and divide it by the annual interest rate of an investment. The resulting figure is the equivalent of the number of years it will take for your investment to double.

If your interest rate is 10%, then your money will double in (72 divided by 10) 7.2 years.

If your interest rate is 6%, then it will take (72 divided by 6) 12 years to double.

At 10%, your original investment doubles every 7.2 years, triples every 11 years, and quadruples every 13 years.

If you invest $750 a year, at 10%, over 20 years, you'll have $42 956.20.

If you invest the same $750 a year, over the same 20 years, but at a 12% interest rate, you'll have $54 039.

Suppose you have your bank automatically transfer $31.25 from your bi-monthly pay cheque into a savings account. That's

$750 a year. There's that $42 956.20 in 20 years, at an average
10% interest rate. There's that $54 039, at 12%. And do you think
you'll really miss that $31.25 per pay cheque?

The Magic of Compounding

Annual Investment	% return	10 years	15 years	20 years	25 years	30 years
$7,500	6	$98,85	$174,570	$275,897	$411,480	$582,235
	8	108,645	203,640	343,215	548,287	849,600
	10	119,527	238,290	429,562	737,602	1,233,675
	12		279,592	540,390	999,975	1,809,975
	14	145,027	328,815	682,680	1,364,025	2,675,850
	16	159,907	387,442	865,275	1,869,075	3,977,325
	18	176,407	457,237	1,099,650	2,569,500	5,932,050
	20	194,685	540,262	1,400,100	3,539,850	8,864,112
Total		**$75,000**	**$112,500**	**$150,000**	**$187,500**	**$225,000**

Compare the results when you invest $ 7,500 each year at various
rates of return. Note the difference that just 2% can make over time.

SCOTIA McLEOD

The Horror of Inflation

Inflation, the amount things go up in cost every year, has been
running at an average 5% per year over the past 30 years. In
other words, the first 5% interest your investment earns simply
means you are breaking even—when inflation is taken into
account.

In the early 1980s, inflation was running at 14% per year.
Your money had to be earning at least that much interest just to
keep from going backwards. (See inflation chart.)

If you're 32 and earning a comfortable $40 000 a year, you'll
have to make $83 157 a year when you're 47 to maintain the
same lifestyle. If, at age 40, you're earning $60 000 a year,
remember you'll have to make $159 198 a year at age 60 to stay
exactly where you are now.

How Inflation Steals Your Money

Your Income with an Inflation Rate of 5%

Your Income Today	Equivalent 5 Years Later	Equivalent 10 Years Later	Equivalent 15 Years Later	Equivalent 20 Years Later
$40,000	$51,051	$65,156	$83,157	$106,132
50,000	63,814	81,445	103,946	132,665
60,000	76,577	97,734	124,736	159,198
70,000	89,340	114,023	145,525	185,731
80,000	102,103	130,312	166,314	212,254
90,000	114,865	146,601	187,104	238,797
100,000	127,622	162,890	207,893	265,330
150,000	191,442	244,344	311,839	397,995
200,000	255,256	325,779	415,786	530,660

SCOTIA McLEOD

The Horror of Taxation

If you are making $30 000 a year or more, then your federal and provincial income tax alone is taking a whopping 30% to 40% off your pay cheque before you see it. Add in all the other taxes (GST, provincial sales taxes, gasoline tax) and Tax Freedom Day, that point in the year when you stop paying the taxman and start paying yourself, arrives sometime in late June or early July.

If you're making $15 000—or about $7 an hour in a full-time job, then the government gives you a break. It takes between 15% and 20% of your income and taxes. But how long do you plan to stay in the $15 000 a year bracket?

If you have not looked for the best return on your investments, then once taxation and inflation have taken their toll, you could end up actually losing money. For example, a 10% return might look attractive, but after 50% tax and 5% inflation, you're just breaking even. A 12% return, after 50% tax and 5% inflation, will give a *real* gain of 1%. In fact, if you can achieve a 1% or 2% return on your investments, after inflation and taxes, you are doing quite well.

The Golden Rules of Saving

1. Paying off your mortgage is the best investment/savings plan you can make. Every $1000 you can put towards reducing your mortgage will generally save you $3000 in interest costs over a 25-year mortgage term.
2. Pay yourself—your investment and savings program—first. Off the top of every paycheque, put a set amount aside for investment. Don't ever dip into your nest egg for anything except the most critical emergency.
3. Start saving early in life. The earlier you accustom yourself to the discipline of saving, the more money you will have when you need it at 55-plus. Never forget the rule of 72. A one-time-only investment of $1000, made when you're 20 and left to accumulate interest at 12% per year, will be worth $64 000 by the time you're 56. The same amount put away at age 40 will be worth $7000 in 16 years.
4. Keep saving, no matter how small the amount. Just $1000 per year, compounding at 10% for 30 years, will give you a grand total of $164 000.
5. This may sound contradictory, but don't be too hard on yourself. Paying off your mortgage, for example, is great. But it's not worth starving yourself to do it.

Learning Financial Discipline:
Ed Patrick

For years and years, Ed Patrick had no budgeting system other than the standard chequing and savings accounts. Although Patrick could never budget on paper, one day he realized he could physically divvy up his paycheque into separate pockets, or accounts. Thanks to automatic bank tellers and unlimited banking services with one monthly fee, Patrick set up nine accounts.

His bi-weekly pay cheque went into his chequing account. Then he transferred set amounts into his car, house, charities, clothes and furniture, children, savings, holiday, and gift accounts. What was left in his chequing account was his spending money until the next pay cheque.

Patrick then had limits to his spending. He couldn't buy a new suit until he had $500 in his clothes account. A once-a-year holiday had to be financed from his holiday account. It took about two years for Patrick to work on the system until it suited him perfectly.

Once the idea of different pockets was deeply instilled in him, Patrick pooled all his accounts into three—chequing, house, and all other accounts. In the "all other accounts," he still kept different accounts, but they were running tallies in the pages of his bank book. That way, he was able to collect much more interest than if the money was in separate pools. The overall result was to bring his financial house into good working order.

He was able to travel, to pay down his mortgage, to save towards a replacement vehicle as well as pay the fuel and main-tenance bills on his current car. Cushions of cash built up in the accounts over the years eased the worry of unexpected bills.

Financial Passages

"Money," said the seven sages of Greece, "is the blood and soul of men. He who has none wanders dead among the living."
—Scipion de Gramont

As you go through life, you are going to have different financial needs at different times.

The only way to retire at 55 is by sticking to a life-long systematic savings plan.

The only way that plan will work is by understanding the different financial stages of your life.

Early Adulthood: Stage I
(18 – 25 years old)

Save for your education. Take a part-time job to finance university or technical school. Houses, stocks, or retirement savings plans come later. You may be able to borrow some money to pay for post-secondary schooling, but rarely will loans—even from parents—cover the entire cost.

An education is worth at least an extra $250 000 in increased wages during your working career. That's money above and beyond what you would make if you went into the workforce with a Grade 12 education. $250 000 … let's see, that could buy a Porsche ($60 000), a yacht ($50 000), a small airplane ($50 000) and a lovely, year-round cottage ($90 000).

The Golden Rules of Stage I
1. Get the best education possible.
2. Save for your education.

Graduation: Stage II
(22 – 30 years old)

Congratulations, you've just graduated from university. You've just landed your first decent job. You want to celebrate—to buy a brand-new car. Buying that car is going to cost you a cool $33 863. Here's proof. You've saved $3000 for transportation. You have a choice. Pay cash for a sturdy clunker, or borrow another $12 000, at 14% interest over five years, to buy the latest Firebird.

If you buy a Firebird, you'll have paid, over five years:

1. Cash down	$3 000
2. $280 a month, loan payments, over 5 years	$16 800
3. Insurance, $1000 a year for 5 years	$5 000
4. Minimal maintenance over 5 years	$1 000
Total:	$25 800

The Firebird is going to cost $25 800.
After five years, you sell the Firebird. It's in good shape. You

get half what you paid for it … $7500.

After five years, then, the car has cost you ($25 800 – 7500) or $18 300.

If you buy the dependable old clunker, over five years you will pay:

1. Full purchase price, cash $3 000
2. Insurance, $500 a year over five years $2 500
3. Maintenance and repairs $500 a year $2 500

The clunker has cost you $8000 over five years. It's still running, and you sell the old beast for half the price you bought it for … $1500. After five years, the clunker has cost $6500 ($8000 – $1500). You save $11 800 ($18 300 for the Firebird, versus $6500 for the clunker).

So where does the other $21 863 come from? Instead of paying off your loan at $280 a month, you could have put that $280 into your own interest-earning investment. If your savings earn you 10% per year, then after five years you'll have actually put aside $16 800, and that will have earned another $5063 in interest. That all adds up to $21 863.

▲ ▲ ▲

At this time, during post-university years, you need only two financial goals: First, if you borrowed to get through school, then you want to pay off that debt. Second, you want to get the cash together for a healthy down payment on a small "starter" home. The mortgage you take out on that home will likely be the best forced savings plan you'll have. You'll also have to buy, and maintain, that sturdy old clunker of a car, and purchase the household essentials for apartment living. You're also allowed some fun. Life can't be all work for the young and restless.

The most important financial decision you can make in Stage II is determining your career. If you have not settled into a career—specialized work commanding a professional salary— by the time you are 30, then you likely won't have one. Without a career, it's terribly difficult to move up the ladder, promotion-wise or financially. Your plan for being financially independent at 55 considerably diminishes.

Work hard to find your career. Take advantage of counselling or self-enhancement courses. Just make sure you've started on your career, or are upgrading yourself towards the right place, by the time you're 30.

The Golden Rules of Stage II
1. Pay off all debts, including education.
2. Save a down payment toward a house.
3. Have a little fun.

First Assets: Stage III
(26 – 35 years old)

As soon as you've put together a 10% down payment, go buy that starter home. You will have the security of home ownership. Your house is an investment that historically has stayed ahead of inflation. Paying a mortgage is, in effect, a forced savings plan. Paying off the principal portion of your mortgage (the original debt) is a wonderful investment because of the amount of money you can save.

As a rule of thumb, you'll pay for your house three times over if you have a standard 25-year-mortgage. Every dollar you put towards the mortgage (on top of your regular payments) is the equivalent of earning three dollars. For example, if you have an $80 000 mortgage and pay $800 a month for five years, then you'll have only reduced the principal owing by 5%, or $4000. The other $44 000 all went towards the interest—into somebody else's pocket, not yours. Many young homeowners engage in an all-out savings plan, in order to put 10% of the value of the mortgage (above the regular payments) towards principal reduction every year.

It's better for most people not to invest in anything else— even a registered retirement savings plan as explained in Chapter 3—besides their own house at this point. A $4000 payment towards principal reduction at the beginning of the $80 000 mortgage cuts five years off the life of the mortgage. That's enormous savings over time. It can't be overstressed. Pay off your mortgage's principal in the biggest chunks you can afford. Financially responsible homeowners aim to have their mortgage paid off within 10 years of purchase. If you've gone the home owner route, you should have your mortgage under control by your mid-30s. If not, retiring at 55 will be more difficult.

There's one other investment you should be making at this stage. Everybody should have some money put aside for emergencies. An emergency fund—the equivalent of about three months' income—means you won't be wiped out by the unforeseen. Once depleted, an emergency fund should be rebuilt.

At this point in life it makes more sense to pay off your mortgage than it does to contribute to an RRSP. When you are young, you usually aren't making as much money as you will later in life. A lower income means a lower tax bracket. You won't save nearly as much now by making RRSP contributions as you will when you're making much more money. When you're younger, you should be concentrating on getting out of debt—so that when you're older, you will have the money to put into tax-saving investments.

The Golden Rules of Stage III
1. Pay off your mortgage.
2. Establish your emergency fund.

Building: Stage IV
(35 – 45 years old)

At 35, you should be well along in your career, have an emergency fund, and have the end of your mortgage in sight. It's time to plan towards retirement. Time to open the RRSP plan, and start maximizing your contributions.

Thanks to inflation, in 15 years you'll need twice the amount you make today to maintain the same standard of living. To be able to retire, you have to start putting aside those tax-free retirement dollars now. If, at 35, you open an RRSP, and continue to make escalating contributions through your most productive years, your RRSP will be fat enough by the time you are 55 to have the option of retiring.

Between 35 and 45, you may want to move into a bigger house. If the first house is paid off, then you'll have a smaller mortgage on house number two. You should have enough spare cash to invest in your RRSP. By this stage, you should be well into your financial education. Learn about the kinds of RRSP investments available. Find a good stockbroker, financial planner, and accountant. Build your financial team.

If you have children, then this is the time to put aside money for their future education. If you do not save for them, early in their lives, then they may not be able to afford the cost of education.

The Golden Rules of Stage IV
1. You will have paid off, or be close to paying off, the mortgage.
2. You shall educate yourself on the various ways of investing within the RRSP.
3. Begin to think of your children's university expenses, and how much you can help.

Peaking: Stage V
(45 – 55 years old)

This is it: the big money decade. You've entered your peak earning years. Your disposable income is at its highest. This is the time you want to develop strong relationships with a good financial advisor, a good accountant, and a good lawyer. The investments you make now are crucial. The results of these financial decisions will determine your standard of living for the rest of your life.

Your focus in this phase is to invest for maximum tax-advantage, putting the maximum, for instance, each year into your RRSP. Many people also purchase their retirement property during this peak income period.

These years are not only your peak *earning* years, but also your peak *saving* years. Usually, living expenses tend to decrease as children leave home, leaving much more money for investment.

If, by the time you reach 55, you have no debts, and the return from your investments equals 60% of your working salary, congratulations. You can retire, if you so choose.

Between the income from your nest egg and pension, you should be able to live comfortably into your twilight years, working or not working, whichever you choose.

The Golden Rules of Stage V
1. Build a sound financial team.
2. Build your RRSP.
3. Invest for maximum tax advantage.
4. Consider purchasing your retirement property.

Retirement: Stage VI
(55 – 65 years old)

Should you retire at 55 or 65, the rules are the same. You're basically concerned with security. You want reasonable certainty that your investments will produce their dividends when you need them, in the amounts you expected. In general, two-thirds of your assets should be in "fixed income" investments— bonds, treasury bills, mortgages, and mortgage-backed securities. The rest can go into good quality stocks or mutual funds. Move your stocks into blue-chip stocks, and transfer your speculative investments into more reliable income-earners. If you continue to work, then you stay on the Stage V plan until you face retirement.

By your late sixties, convert most of your remaining stocks and investments into guaranteed income-producers. Change your RRSPs into Registered Retirement Income Funds or annuities. All you want is sufficient cash-flow to maintain the lifestyle you now have for the rest of your life.

Estate planning is a must, so the taxman won't take everything that should go to your heirs.

Finally, go out and have some fun. After working hard all those years, and being so careful with your money, you deserve it.

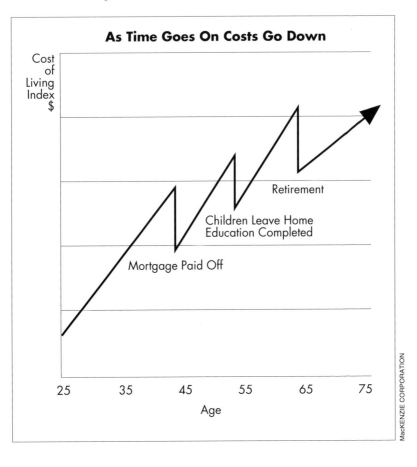

The Golden Rules of Stage VI

1. Gradually convert your investments into guaranteed income-earners.
2. Convert your RRSPs into retirement income funds or annuities.
3. Update your will.
4. Plan for your estate.
5. Have some fun. You have earned it.

Registered Retirement Savings Plans

I don't like money, actually, but it quiets my nerves.

—Joe Lewis

To encourage Canadians to save towards their own retirement, the government allows us to put aside a certain percentage of our income every year. You do not pay tax on the savings you put into a Registered Retirement Savings Plan (RRSP), or on the interest those savings earn, until you take the money out of the plan. You can let your savings grow without paying tax. But you must understand that RRSPs are not a tax-avoidance scheme. You will pay tax on RRSP savings the day you begin to withdraw

money from the RRSP. In other words, the $1000 you put in this year, along with all the interest it will earn in the years to come, won't be taxed until you take the money out of the RRSP sometime in the future. You are earning interest, in effect, on money that otherwise you would have paid in tax.

You will eventually pay taxes on your RRSP money. But it's likely you'll take the money out of the plan at a time when you are earning less money than you are now. And you will have accumulated all that tax-free interest as well.

Why an RRSP?

The effects of having interest compound without tax are quite dramatic. The example assumes a 50% marginal tax rate, and a 10% growth rate.

	1990	2000	2010
A. Invest $5,000 in an RRSP	$5,000	$12,969	$33,637
After withdrawal		$ 6,484	$16,818
B. Do not put the $5,000 in an RRSP, so you are taxed on it immediately	$2,500	$ 4,072	$ 6,633

SCOTIA McLEOD

An RRSP is nothing more than a special account, labeled for government reporting purposes.

It might be an account at a bank or trust company. It might be a "self-directed" account through a brokerage firm. Within that account, you can have guaranteed investment certificates, mutual funds, stocks, and so on. You can even, with some conditions, make a mortgage to yourself. Think of RRSPs as your very own security blanket. One thing became clear during the 1980s. As our governments struggle to reduce massive debt, it's no longer a safe bet to assume they will be able to care for us in our retirement years.

RRSPs come with rules.

For people without a company pension plan, the most money you can put into RRSPs for 1992 is either 18% of your 1991 "earned" income (usually less than your salaried income) or $12 500, whichever is less. Starting in 1994, the maximum amount you can put into an RRSP will increase by $1000 per year until 1996, when it will level off at $15 500 ... or 18% of your income, whichever is less.

If you have a company pension plan, then the rules are more complicated. Each year, Revenue Canada will tell you how much money you can put in your RRSP. Revenue Canada will give you a very important number known as your "PA," or pension adjustment. You can also find your pension adjustment figure on your last T4 slip, in box 52. Once you have your PA number, calculating your annual RRSP limit is easy. First, calculate whichever is less: 18% of your earned income, or $12 500. Then subtract your pension adjustment from this number. The difference is the maximum amount you can put into your RRSP that year.

Beginning in 1991, if you don't use up all your eligible RRSP contributions in one year, then you can go back and use them for up to seven years in the future. Say in 1991 you didn't have any extra money to invest in your RRSP. But in 1992, you had lots of extra money. You are allowed to make up for the contribution that you missed the year before—within certain limits.

In addition, you can over-contribute to your RRSP up to a lifetime limit of $8000. This amount can be left in your RRSP to be used as a deduction in some future year. One word of caution. Since this $8000 is more than your contribution limit (you can't claim it on your tax return), it's money you've already paid taxes on. If you don't use it up as part of future RRSP deductions, you'll pay tax on it again when you withdraw it from the RRSP. You'll end up being taxed twice on the $8000.

Once you've put money into your RRSP, you cannot take it out, unless you're prepared to share it with the taxman. If you take money out of an RRSP, then you must add that amount to your taxable income for the year.

Tax-deferral is your ticket to a financially comfortable retirement. If you invest $3500 a year, over 25 years, into an RRSP earning an average interest of 12% per year, you'll have $466 654 in your nest egg. If you invest the same money outside an RRSP, and declare the interest as taxable income at the time of cashing in that investment, you'll wind up with $209 093. The government would, depending on your income bracket, tax your profits at a 45% tax rate.

We cannot overstress how important it is to save as much as you can, especially in your RRSP. As a general rule of thumb, if you don't save more than you think you'll need in retirement, then you won't save enough.

RRSPs, however, are not necessarily the be-all and end-all, especially if you're in your 20s or early-30s, are committed to a large mortgage, and are not yet in the top-tax bracket. In this case, ignore the siren call of RRSPs, and continue to put most of your savings towards paying off the mortgage. Nobody ever

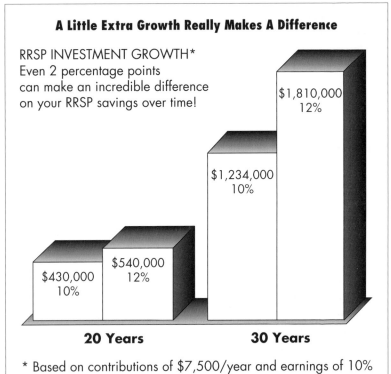

A Little Extra Growth Really Makes A Difference

RRSP INVESTMENT GROWTH*
Even 2 percentage points
can make an incredible difference
on your RRSP savings over time!

$1,810,000
12%

$1,234,000
10%

$540,000
12%

$430,000
10%

20 Years   **30 Years**

* Based on contributions of $7,500/year and earnings of 10%
vs. 12% over 20 & 30 years.

SCOTIA McLEOD

went terribly wrong with the battle cry of the middle class: "Pay down the mortgage!"

Money used to "buy down" a high-interest mortgage rate (reducing the principal faster than the set-out payment schedule) is by far the best "reverse" savings you can do. By paying off your mortgage earlier than planned, you'll be saving thousands upon thousands of dollars. It's usually a better investment than an RRSP, even with its tax savings.

Shop around for RRSPs. Different financial institutions have different fee structures, types of investments, and rates of return.

Designing Your Own RRSP

Once you know what you're doing financially, an RRSP of the "self-directed" variety can often earn greater returns than "regular" RRSPs that offer a fixed interest rate. The difference between a self-directed RRSP and a regular RRSP is that you control your own investments. You can purchase stocks, bonds, or mutual funds.

Your self-directed RRSP is usually an account held through a financial institution—a stockbroker, a bank, a trust company—into which you would deposit your annual RRSP contribution.

You can invest in your own mortgage, and you are allowed to invest a portion of your self-directed RRSP in non-Canadian investments. Currently in 1992, 16% of your RRSP can go into non-Canadian investments. That amount will increase to 18% in 1993 and to 20% in 1994. About the only things you are not allowed to invest in, under RRSP rules, are physical assets like gold, cars, or paintings.

There is but one golden rule in taking personal control of your RRSP destiny: Be cautious.

Your RRSP account should follow the investment "pyramid" rules spelled out in Chapter 5. The bulk of your money should be safe in the foundation of the pyramid, in "interest-bearing" investments—investments where a steady stream of interest income is compounding away, guaranteeing a slow but steady return. Examples of interest-bearing investments are guaranteed investment certificates, government bonds, term deposits, or treasury bills. Remember, this is your retirement fund. You don't want to gamble with your future.

There's another reason for placing most of your interest-bearing investments into your RRSP. Generally, Revenue Canada imposes a higher rate of taxation on interest income than on any other investment gain. From the government's point of view, the low-risk investment is considered fair game for full taxation. It makes sense, then, to place those low-risk investments in your RRSP plan.

Be careful: There's nothing to stop you but your own foolishness in a self-directed RRSP. A fast-talking con-artist could talk you into investing in a "sure" thing. Nothing stops you from selling all your other investments in your RRSP, and replacing them with two million shares of Can't Possibly Fail penny stock.

Nevertheless, if you manage your account properly, and take the advice of your stockbroker or financial advisor (see Chapter 12 on choosing your financial team), then you are likely to earn a substantially greater rate of return on your self-directed RRSP than through a normal RRSP.

Financing Your Own Mortgage through Your RRSP

Yes, it can be done. You can make a mortgage to yourself through an RRSP. Say you manage to accumulate $100 000 in your RRSP, and still have a $60 000 mortgage on your house. Your mortgage, generally speaking, costs a few percentage points more than the percentage of interest your RRSP earns.

You can, through a trust company, pay off the existing mortgage with funds from your RRSP, then make out a mortgage to yourself and place it, as one of your assets, in your RRSP. Those payments are made to your own RRSP, not to another lender. You are paying yourself back at a better rate than you can earn through normal investments.

The rules say your RRSP mortgage has to be set at the going rate. You can't lower your own mortgage interest rate to an unrealistically low level. You need to have at least $30 000 to $40 000 to make a self-directed RRSP mortgage pay. The extra fees charged by trust companies to administer your mortgage eat up any advantage if the amount is less.

Using Your RRSP to Buy a Home

The federal government has introduced a Home Buyer's Plan.

Under the plan, you can withdraw up to $20 000 tax free from your RRSP to actually buy your own home.

The money has to be paid back to your RRSP, in equal annual installments, over 15 years. You can also pay ahead of schedule. You are not required to make interest payments on what is in effect an interest-free loan to yourself from your own RRSP.

The current program expires on March 1 1994.

There are two conditions to the Home Buyer's Plan. Should you take advantage of the plan, RRSP contributions between December 2, 1992 and March 2, 1994 will be disallowed. And if you can't meet the annual repayment, you'll face a tax penalty. The money you cannot repay is considered to be permanently withdrawn from the RRSP.

Other Uses of Your RRSP

An RRSP doesn't have to be exclusively geared towards your retirement, although retirement income is its primary focus. It can be used in a number of ways to "average out" your income for tax purposes.

You can, for instance, invest in your wife's or husband's RRSP. Suppose your spouse is working, but at a significantly lower salary than yours. One of you may be planning on being a full-time parent, once you have two or more young children. You can put money into your mate's RRSP, as long as your total contribution to both RRSPs doesn't go over the maximum allowed to you. If the money has been in your spouse's RRSP for three years minimum, your spouse can withdraw it, and call it his or her own, for income tax purposes. Your partner will pay a far lower rate of taxation on the withdrawn money than you would.

The major income earner can make contributions to the other spouse's RRSP, towards the goal of having equal amounts of money in both plans. This makes for a big tax saving down the line. Instead of one of you taking out $60 000 from your RRSP and paying $20 000 to $25 000 in taxes, two of you are withdrawing $30 000 each, and paying $7000 each in taxes.

Your RRSP can be used as an income-leveller for yourself. Suppose you're an oil rigger. One year you might earn $70 000. The next year, the bottom falls out of the oil patch, and you might earn $20 000.

You can take money out of your taxable income in the high-earning years, and put it into your RRSP. In a lean year, you can take it out of your RRSP, and it won't be taxed at nearly as high a level, since you'll have less overall taxable income.

Slowly but Surely:
Michael Baker

Michael Baker is where we all hope to be when we're 61. When the accountant was but a young man of 27, the federal government introduced RRSPs—in 1957. The first year, you could invest 10% of your income, up to a maximum of $1500. Baker just didn't have that kind of available cash. But he did come up with $400 a year. Slowly but surely, over a number of years, he was able to contribute the maximum allowable. As it accumulated interest, as dividends were returned on stocks, and stocks appreciated, Baker's very conservatively invested RRSP money was not taxed. Now, as he begins to shift his attention to post-retirement taxation matters, Baker has a $337 000 RRSP "war chest."

Mortgages

Pay off the mortgage!

—Rallying cry of the middle class

Welcome to the biggest financial commitment you are ever likely to make.

You are going to walk into your friendly neighbourhood bank or trust company, look the manager straight in the eye, and ask for a loan worth at least four times as much as your annual salary. The manager probably won't bat an eyelid. As long as you agree, under law, that the bank will own your house if you can't meet the mortgage payments.

Mortgages are used to purchase real estate, in this case, your home.

Your banker agrees to give you a loan worth 75% to 90% of the current value of your house. It's a loan that has a surprisingly low rate of interest compared to normal consumer loans … up to two or three percentage points less. But it's a loan

that will take a good chunk of your life to pay. The average "amortization" period of a mortgage—the time period over which the entire mortgage is to be paid back—is usually 25 years: 300 months.

Why, you ask, would bankers dare commit to a certain interest rate over 25 years, given the enormous variation in interest rates over the years? They don't. They agree with you on the total amortization period of the mortgage—the number of years it will take to pay it all back. Then they proceed to set the "term," the number of years at which the interest rate you've agreed upon will be in effect.

At the end of that time-period, or term, the interest rate is re-established according to current market interest rates. You go back to see your banker every time your term—from six months to five years—is renewed.

State of Shock

First-time mortgage holders usually go into a state of shock when, after a number of years, they "renew" their mortgage. Having paid a large sum every month towards their mortgage, they discover they have hardly made a dent in the principal (the amount still left to be paid).

In the first 4 or 5 years of a 25-year mortgage, 94% of the monthly payment is going towards interest—the money the bank is charging you for lending you that huge loan.

"Paying down" the mortgage as quickly as possible is an excellent investment, especially for your own financial security. On top of your fixed monthly payments you should strive to make "principal-reduction" payments (chunks of money given to your mortgage holder to reduce the mortgage amount). Paying off your principal as fast as possible will save the equivalent of years and years of future salary.

Very few people manage to save the $80 000 to $180 000 it costs—depending on the part of the country you live in—to pay for a pleasant "starter" home. Most of us work very hard just to save the 10% down payment usually required by lenders to buy our first home.

Why Buy?

You have a choice. Either you're paying rent—living in somebody else's property—or paying a bit more than the rent to make an investment in yourself. Paying off the house mortgage as fast as possible is probably the best "forced-savings" plan you can have. Once you fully own your home, or at least have the mortgage down to manageable proportions, you'll have the most solid asset possible in your investment portfolio. There is also the invaluable sense of security and sense of place that comes from owning a mortgage-free home.

Some financial advisors say paying off your mortgage is not the best way to invest your earnings. They may have a financial point. But they discount the value of security. Once you've paid off the mortgage on your home, you'll always have a roof over your head.

That said, a word of caution: For conservative reasons, you may not be financially ready to buy a house. Bankers believe, and it's a good rule-of-thumb, that ongoing house costs should not exceed 32% of your family's gross income. If the monthly mortgage, taxes, insurance, utilities, and maintenance costs, on careful calculation, add up to more than 32% of your family's income, you could be running the grave danger of getting in over your head before you start ... even if you have enough money for a down payment.

Remember, if you're a first-time buyer, that this will be your starter house, your first home, not your dream home. Pay for the bungalow, then upgrade as your financial situation allows.

Mortgage Options

Mortgages are like cars: You pick the size you can afford, then decide on the options.

1. A "closed" or "open" mortgage
A closed mortgage allows you to make regular payments (as on standard mortgage tables) with limits on how much more you can pay towards the principal before the end of the mortgage term. (Standard closed mortgages allow you to pay off a maximum 10% of the principal outstanding each calendar year.)

A closed mortgage agreement often contains a prepayment penalty.

An open mortgage lets you pay off the principal whenever you want. If you won a lottery, you could walk in the next day and pay off the entire $100 000 balance outstanding without paying any penalty.

Most people choose a closed mortgage. It's usually cheaper (1/2%to 1% lower interest rate) than the open mortgage and it still allows you to pay down the principal by 10% per year. In any case, a closed mortgage can be reduced by any amount at the time of the term renewal.

2. "Fixed" versus "variable" interest rates

A fixed rate is the interest rate you agree to pay for the term of your mortgage. Suppose you agree to an 11% interest rate over a two-year term. No matter what happens to the market interest rate in those two years, whether the standard interest rate for mortgages goes up or down, you will have the same monthly payment as agreed upon.

A variable interest rate, however, can go up and down like a yo-yo. It's governed by whatever the interest rate happens to be. If interest rates drop, then a variable interest rate is great because your payments drop immediately. If interest rates rise dramatically (anything is possible), then you could suddenly find yourself facing a much heftier monthly payment than you had ever budgeted for.

Since most mortgage-holders tend to budget to the maximum when planning monthly payments, most people opt for a fixed interest rate over a one- to five-year term. The last thing they can afford is a nasty monthly surprise: an increase in their mortgage payments the month before Christmas.

3. A short versus a long term mortgage

"Term" is the 1- to 10-year period within the 25-year amortization where the same mortgage payment is made each month based on an agreed-upon interest rate.

The length of term is a matter of judgment. Generally, when interest rates are low, homeowners opt for a five year or longer term. If interest rates rise during that time, then they are protected. But a small premium must be paid, in the form of a slightly higher interest rate, for the guarantee of a stable monthly payment.

If interest rates are high, and the financial world believes they will fall soon, then it may be wise to take a short-term mortgage. The hope is that interest rates will be lower when the mortgage is renewed, six months to a year later.

4. A "short" versus a "long" amortization period
Amortization is the time frame within which a mortgage must be entirely paid off. Traditionally, in the mortgage industry, mortgages are amortized over 25 years.

You have a choice. You can opt for an amortization period as short as you want, to get the mortgage paid off in a hurry. Or you can pay your mortgage off slowly over 25 years.

Most people don't go for the shortened amortization period. When you originally buy your house, you're usually stretching your budget to the limit to meet the monthly payment over a 25-year amortization.

Let's say you want to take out a mortgage for $50 000, at a 13% interest rate. If the amortization period was the standard 25 years, you'd be paying back $551.20 a month in principal and interest.

If you took the 5-year amortization period, then you would commit yourself to paying double the monthly mortgage payment you would make over 25 years. But you'd be free of the extra 20 years' worth of payments.

Interest on Your Mortgage

Over 20 years	Over 15 years	Over 10 years	Over 5 years
$573.75 a month	$621.50 a month	$736.50 a month	$1129 a month
Total $137, 700	Total $111, 870	Total $88, 380	Total $67, 740

SCOTIA McLEOD

5. Paying off the mortgage

Once you know how much monthly payment you must make, you can start saving to pay off the mortgage.

Just because you signed papers in which you promise to make large payments every month for the foreseeable future, you haven't necessarily committed yourself to life-long debtor status. In fact, if you wish to "accelerate the paydown of principal" (paying off the mortgage) then you'll be like most Canadians. We're among the most industrious homeowners in the world. The average Canadian couple usually pays off their mortgage in 11 years even though they invariably begin by opting for the 25-year amortization period.

As mentioned, most "closed" mortgages still allow the right to pay down the amount of principal outstanding by 10% per year. If your mortgage is sitting at $70 000 or $80 000, this is a large amount of disposable income to put together for one lump-sum debt repayment per year. However, if you manage to meet that 10% pay-down of your mortgage each year, then you will save tens of thousands of dollars—a truly staggering amount.

Because lenders are very competitive, the banks and other institutions have come up with dozens of ways to help you pay off your mortgage more quickly. For example, instead of paying once a month (12 payments a year), you can pay every week, every 2 weeks, or every 4 weeks. The bank adjusts your payment so you are paying off the principal more quickly than the original agreement.

Let common sense be your guiding principle. Settle for a monthly payment you know you can handle, and then do your best to accelerate your payments in whatever form is best suited to your financial affairs.

Golden Rules of Handling a Mortgage

1. **Pay it off:** Try to reduce the principal by at least 10% per year. You'll pay off the mortgage in one-third the time. Never forget the great rallying cry of the middle class: "Pay off the mortgage!"
2. **Ante up at purchase time:** Try to raise as much cash as you can for the down payment. The bigger the down payment, the better off you are in the long run.

3. **Remember the extras:** Don't forget, when you are purchasing a home, that the legal, appraisal, land title, and survey fees are all costly. Make sure you budget for those costs.
4. **Read the fine print:** Check carefully into all the costs associated with transferring or starting up your mortgage. It's usually not worthwhile to move your mortgage from company to company, unless there are substantial savings involved.

Clear Title to a Dream Home:
Tony Vickers

Tony Vickers is 40 years old. He's a carpenter with a Grade 9 education. His 2750-square foot home has a sunroom, a library, a sewing room, a jacuzzi, a playroom, and a huge lot. It's also mortgage-free.

Vickers didn't win a lottery. He didn't run into any windfall profits. In 1975, he bought his first home, a rowhouse condominium, for $28 000—$11 000 cash, $17 000 mortgage. An industrious sort, Vickers took side jobs whenever he could. Every time he had an extra $15, $25, $50, he marched down to his mortgage company and put a bit more towards reduction of the principal owing on his mortgage. It worked. He paid off that mortgage inside three years. Once the mortgage was gone, Vickers sold the condo (for $40 000) in 1978. His next home was a small bungalow, 1100 square feet. It needed work. He paid $77 000; $40 000 cash from the first home and $37 000 in a mortgage.

Tony went to work. He poured the concrete pad and built a double garage, redid the basement, built a fence, put in shrubs. None of the improvements were expensive. They all added to the house's value.

His mortgage company knew him well. Once again, Tony would trot in every time he had an extra $50 in his pocket. He knew each $50 put toward reducing the size of the mortgage would save $150 down the line in interest costs. Three years later, the small bungalow was paid off. That same year, 1981, Tony sold the improved property for $124 000, at the peak of the real estate market. By this time, Tony and his wife had two

young children and a dog. He upgraded again, paying
$170 000— $124 000 cash from the sale of his last home, plus a
$46 000 mortgage. The carpenter stuck to the same formula—
improve the property by his own efforts and pay down the
mortgage whenever possible. Thanks to the recession that
stalked Alberta through the mid-1980s, it took Tony five years
to pay off this one.

By the time he was mortgage-free, the real estate market was
in deep doldrums. Tony didn't panic. He held on to the house.
At the same time, he opened an account at his bank that he
called the "bigger home fund." That's where he put every extra
cent he made for three more years. By 1989, things looked a little
less grim in Alberta, and the real estate market began to recover.
He sold for $175 000—hardly a major capital gain considering
he'd paid $170 000 eight years before. But, again, he had paid
off the mortgage, and he was buying in the same city. At the
same time, Vickers had $65 000 in his bigger home fund. So
when the house of his family's dreams showed up on the market, for $235 000, Vickers could pay 100%. At 40, Vickers had the
home of his dreams. And he didn't owe a cent to anybody.

Making Your Money Work for You

To know value is to know the meaning of the market.
—Charles Dow

You've almost paid off your house. The end of your mortgage is in sight. Now you can start to place your savings in other investments besides the home front.

There is one fundamental rule to investing: Risk is equal to reward ... reward equals risk.

Look at the interest rates offered by all the banks and trust companies in your area (usually listed periodically in the business section of your local newspaper). They're all within a half percentage point of each other.

The "market" usually agrees on the guaranteed "benchmark" return on an investment that has no risk. Investment houses believe they can earn that rate of return for their customers without difficulty.

"Penny stocks" represent the other investment extreme. Penny stocks go up and down. One day, a penny stock might be worth two cents; the next day, ten cents; the third day, back down to one cent. Fortunes can be made or lost within hours in this very risky investment area.

If an investment can increase astronomically in value, there's an equally good chance it can drop to zero value in the same time span. There's high risk for the investor, but also the chance of a high reward.

The Investment Pyramid

As you begin to make investments outside of your mortgage, you'll be building a financial house as sturdy as that of an Egyptian pyramid: Rock-solid with a big foundation at the bottom, getting smaller towards its point.

Most of your money should be at the base of the pyramid, in risk-free investments—investments that automatically gather interest, and are "guaranteed" by the federal government or the government's Canadian Depositors' Insurance Corporation. The rest of your money can be divided up, in diminishing percentages, from bottom to top, in riskier and riskier investments.

At the base of your pyramid you have assets such as your house, guaranteed investment certificates, Canada Savings Bonds, emergency funds, pensions, treasury bills, and term deposits.

At the top of the pyramid, you might toss $1000 into that high-flying gold stock your wheeler-dealer friend told you was a sure winner. If it works, you sell in a week at $2000. If it fizzles, well, you hadn't invested your life's savings.

Every time you consider any investment, you must weigh its level of risk. See if it fits into your pyramid at the right level, without distorting your pyramid's shape.

The pyramid is absolutely critical to any conservative saver/investor. Ignore it at your peril.

Risk and Your Investment Pyramid

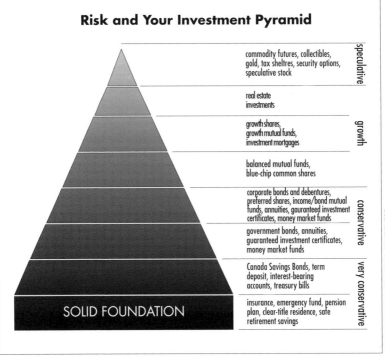

commodity futures, collectibles, gold, tax sheltres, security options, speculative stock — *speculative*

real estate investments

growth shares, growth mutual funds, investment mortgages — *growth*

balanced mutual funds, blue-chip common shares

corporate bonds and debentures, preferred shares, income/bond mutual funds, annuities, gauranteed investment certificates, money market funds — *conservative*

government bonds, annuities, guaranteed investment certificates, money market funds

Canada Savings Bonds, term deposit, interest-bearing accounts, treasury bills — *very conservative*

SOLID FOUNDATION

insurance, emergency fund, pension plan, clear-title residence, safe retirement savings

2000 A.D. GUIDE TO FINANCIAL AWARENESS

Investing for Assured Income

One thousand dollars left to earn interest at 8% a year will grow to 43 quadrillion dollars in 400 years, but the first 100 years are the hardest.
—Sidney Homer

Interest-earning investments—those investments promising to pay a fixed percentage return for the use of your money—are the safest way of making your money work for you. They also give you the lowest rate of return on your money compared to the other available investments. But they do protect your capital.

Canada Savings Bonds

There's no investment like a Canada Savings Bond (CSB). You can buy a CSB through any bank, trust company, or stockbroker in amounts as small as $100. You can cash them in anytime, at most financial institutions. They can be converted to cash as easily as a withdrawal from a savings account.

In October, the federal government puts its yearly offering of CSBs up for sale to the general public. It announces the interest rate for the coming year on the new issue, and for all the bonds still outstanding.

CSBs can only be sold to individuals. They can't be bought or sold to anybody else. The only alternative to keeping bonds is to cash them in.

You can buy bonds that pay regular interest every November 1, or bonds that compound the interest—automatically adding the interest to the amount of the bond.

Bonds are one of the biggest ways the Canadian government raises cash. In the last few years, offerings of $8-$9 billion, the equivalent of Manitoba's entire provincial budget, have been snapped up by the public in weeks.

CSBs are an excellent way of earning good interest on your emergency fund, and almost always pay more interest than savings accounts.

Treasury Bills

Every week, representatives from brokerage firms, banks, and trust companies submit sealed bids to the Bank of Canada. They are bidding on the almost $1 billion a week the federal government "sells" to the public through the financial vehicle known as Treasury Bills, or T-Bills.

The Bank of Canada "sells" (actually borrows) as much money as the government requires for its overspending habits each week. They start with the highest bid, then keep accepting lower bids until they have raised the money the government needs. Basically, the financial community is lending the government of Canada money for its short-term needs.

Because the smallest unit sold is $100 000, institutions rather than individuals usually buy T-Bills. Brokerage firms buy T-Bills, then break them down into bite-sized chunks for sale to their clients. A broker might buy $1 million worth of T-Bills, then sell $10 000 units to individuals with a predetermined interest rate. T-Bills mature in 30, 60, 180, or 360 days.

T-Bills, unlike CSBs, can be bought and sold by anybody. A huge secondary market for T-Bills exists. You can pick and choose from a large variety of T-Bills being offered at any time on the financial market.

Guaranteed Investment Certificates
(GICs)

Guaranteed investment certificates, or GICs, offer a set amount of interest in return for the use of your money, for terms of up to five years.

The catch is that you cannot normally cash them in before the term is up without paying a penalty for the premature withdrawal.

GICs can be bought at any time for amounts as small as $100. Normally, the longer you lock your money in, the better the interest rate you'll get.

You may choose to buy a certificate that pays out the interest as often as every month or one that compounds the interest to maturity.

GICs are a simple, easy investment with a competitive yield. The government's Canadian Depositors' Insurance Corporation guarantees your GIC, to a limit of $60 000 per individual, per institution. If the trust company goes broke, then you will still be paid out in full.

The only disadvantage is that you must lock in your money.

National Housing Association Mortgages
(NHA Mortgages)

Trust companies and banks have now set up a way that you can invest directly in mortgages.

The financial institution takes investors' money and pools it into a limited number of residential mortgages, all guaranteed by the Canada Mortgage and Housing Corporation (that is, the Government of Canada).

Through the pool, you become a mortgage lender. You'll be paid back, just like the bank, in monthly payments that include principal and interest. Each mortgage pool consists of 20 to 50 registered mortgages.

If one of the mortgage payers defaults, your payments are not interrupted. The mortgage and housing corporation has guaranteed your NHA pool, and will automatically step in and pick up the mortgage payments of the defaulter. The CMHC guarantees the entire mortgage, no matter what the amount.

Like T-Bills, NHA mortgages can be bought and sold. You can buy and sell and even speculate in the NHA pools. The price changes, because the market dictates the supply and demand for such a security.

NHA mortgages are excellent investments for those of you who want a steady monthly income from your investment. If you want to cash in your investment, you can sell your NHA mortgages in the financial marketplace.

Bonds

There's much more to the world of bonds than CSBs (Canada Savings Bonds). Bonds are promissory notes issued by private corporations and the three levels of government—municipal, provincial, and federal. They are sold to the general public through brokerage firms.

Bonds offer competitive interest rates comparable to, or slightly higher than, GICs (guaranteed investment certificates). They are sold in $1000 units, over terms of 2 to 30 years.

Bonds don't compound your interest. Once or twice a year, you receive an interest payment. If you actually possess the bond certificate itself, you might see interest coupons (detachable coupons that are cashed in as they come due). If your bond is held at a brokerage firm, then the interest is credited to your account. Other types of bonds mail you the interest directly.

The interest rate on a bond is determined by investor confidence in the company or government. Usually government bonds, by their very security, offer lower interest rates. The "blue chip" company offering a good quality bond will sell its bonds at a higher rate than government bonds. A company making its first bond "offering" on the market will usually offer a better interest rate than established companies, to attract investors.

In Canada, bonds are rated by two independent rating services: the Dominion Bond Rating Service, and the Canadian Bond Rating Service. They both publish booklets evaluating Canadian bond offerings.

Private sector bonds have to be backed by specifically defined assets of the company. If the company goes bankrupt, then the bond-holders would have first call on that asset, or on the bond's "collateral," to salvage what value they could for their bonds.

Corporate bonds are backed basically by investor confidence in a company. The less established or more financially insecure the company, the higher the interest rate must be on its bonds in order to attract investment.

An astute investor can buy blue-chip corporate bonds that are almost as safe as, and earn more interest than, their government counterparts.

Government-issued bonds are the best place to put large sums of money for safe-keeping and steady interest income over the long term. It's the only investment (besides NHA mortgage pools) where more than $60 000 is guaranteed. The government has to go bankrupt before its bonds would be endangered.

Debentures

A debenture is a very simple thing. A debenture is simply a promissory note backed by nothing more than the company's promise to pay. They're riskier than bonds. If the company went bankrupt, then the debenture holder could end up with nothing. So debentures usually offer a slightly higher interest rate than bonds. They are, in fact, a more common method of raising long-term cash for private corporations than bonds.

The Bond Market

Every bond and debenture can be bought or sold during its long march to maturity, leading to a roaring business in the "secondary" bond/debenture market.

If interest rates drop below the interest rate at which the bond was issued (most bond interest rates remain fixed for the life of the bond) then the bond has added resale value.

If interest rates skyrocket above the interest rate your bond is offering, then the bond's immediate value drops.

Buying and selling bonds can be profitable when interest rates are fluctuating. Predicting whether interest rates will rise or fall is a risky business. Speculators buy bonds hoping that their predictions will prove correct. This risk doesn't seem to affect the nerves of bond buyers and sellers. Thirty times more money changes hands in the Canadian bond markets than in Canada's stock exchanges.

While trading bonds is risky, the purchase of a bond with the intention of hanging on to it until its maturity is not ... unless the government or company issuing the bond collapses.

Bonds offer interest rates as good as or better than GICs. They pay that interest once or twice a year. If you need to cash them in immediately, then you can sell them on the bond market, as long as you're willing to accept the price of the day for your particular bond.

Types of Bonds

The market has a myriad of variations on the basic bond. Three examples are "retractable" bonds/debentures, "extendable" bonds, and "convertible" debentures.

"Retractable" bonds/debentures offer two different maturity dates. You have the option to cash in your bond at full price on either of the two maturity dates.

"Extendable" bonds also have two maturity dates. But, unless otherwise notified, the company will automatically cash in the bond at its first date of maturity.

Finally, there are "convertible" debentures, debentures that can be "converted" into a specific number of common shares in the same company over a given time period.

Because their value is tied to the fortune of the company's common stock, the trading value of convertible debentures is unstable. If the stock is rising, then the debentures are worth more. If they drop, then the debentures are worth less.

Buying convertible debentures is a good introduction to the stock market. You have the choice of "converting" the debentures into stocks—if the stock is doing well—or keeping the debenture if the stock is low, and still collecting the debenture's interest.

The biggest investment phenomenon of the 1980s was "junk" bonds—bonds offering a very high interest rate—issued by companies with very low credit ratings. Because the interest rates were so high (over 20%), investors snapped up junk bonds. But the junk bond buyer took the chance that these financially unstable companies could go bankrupt, leaving the bonds worthless. In fact, many of those companies did go bankrupt. As many as half the junk bonds sold may ultimately be worthless.

Coupons

Coupons are the twice-yearly interest payments that come in the form of detachable "coupons" when you purchase a bond. A brokerage firm will buy a $100 000 bond, tear off all the interest coupons, and sell them individually. A $5000 coupon, coming due in one year, might sell for $4550. A $5000 coupon due in three years might fetch $3700. A $5000 coupon maturing in 2010 might sell for $500. The longer before a coupon comes due, the less you pay for it today. You don't receive any interest until the coupon matures. Then you get it all in one lump sum.

Coupons are a tremendous investment for an RRSP. You can plan ahead, buying coupons that will mature as you need cash. There's no reinvestment hassle, no worry about collecting the interest or reinvesting small amounts of dollars. You get the full value of compounding—your $500 investment will be worth $5000 in 22 years. Coupons that come off bonds issued by federal and provincial governments are a very safe investment. If, for an unexpected reason, you must sell, there is an active market for coupons.

Preferred Shares

"Preferred" shares are different from the normal "common" shares you buy and sell in stock markets. (See the section called "The Stock Market" in Chapter 7 for a discussion of common shares.)

Preferred shares usually don't fluctuate very much in value. They're attractive because they pay a "dividend," usually a quarterly payment, issued to shareholders by the company every three months. All preferred shares are sold with the provision that the company can, at a future date, buy back the shares.

Dividends reap a little extra return on your investment thanks to government taxation policy.

Back in the days when most Canadians thought the only safe place to put savings was in the bank, the government decided to encourage Canadians to invest in the stock market by introducing a tax-break on dividend income.

You pay about 25% less tax on income that comes from dividends than on income that comes from interest-earning investments. This tax break makes preferred shares competitive with bonds and guaranteed investment certificates. Preferred shares normally pay a slightly lower return than the going market rate on those other fixed-income investments, but the tax break usually gives you a better after-tax return.

Preferred shares tend to be far more stable in price than common shares. You don't invest in "preferreds," as they are called, for price appreciation. You invest for that lightly taxed dividend.

Preferreds come in a variety of sizes and shapes. The dividend from "floating rate preferred shares" will "float" or change depending on current interest rates.

When you purchase a "retractable" preferred share, the company agrees to buy back the preferred share at a fixed price in the future, even if the share's market price has dropped.

"Convertible" preferred shares pay a dividend. They also can be exchanged for common shares in the same company.

One word of caution. Preferred shares may, ever so slowly, disappear. The government seems to have decided Canadians are investing in the financial marketplace at such a clip that tax breaks for preferred shares are no longer needed. The government is slowly lowering the tax break on dividend income. That tax break is important. It gives preferred shares a better return than bonds, with very little additional risk. There is still a large preferred share market. But not quite so many preferred shares are being sold by companies. And many companies are buying back their old preferred shares. If the tax break is totally eliminated, then the value of preferred shares, usually reliable, will probably drop.

Taking Care of Retirement:
Jane Manson

Jane Manson couldn't believe her luck. She won a Big Sisters dream home at a charity raffle. Manson was 49, a secretary, and single. She hadn't been able to save towards her retirement. She immediately sold the dream home for $162 000. She paid off the $58 000 mortgage still remaining on her house. Still, the remaining $104 000 was not enough for Manson to retire. Her broker bought coupons stripped from Government of Canada bonds. Valued at $104 000, they would mature in 11 years, giving Manson a return at that time of $327 000. While she had too much to be placed immediately into an RRSP, Manson was able to roll a few coupons into her RRSP each year leading up to her retirement. With this move, at no risk, Manson had taken care of her retirement.

Investing for Growth

The market, like The Lord, helps those who help themselves. But, unlike The Lord, the market does not forgive those who know not what they do.

　　　　　　　　　　　　　　　　　—Warren Buffett

Mutual Funds

A mutual fund is a pool of money put together by individual investors, invested by professional managers. The money is entrusted to the expertise of the mutual fund's managers. They attempt to earn a higher rate of return on your cash than you could by investing on your own.

　　If you look in the financial section of any Canadian newspaper, you'll see the "mutual fund" section on its own, separate from stock market reports. The report lists just one figure for every mutual fund; that figure being the price it cost that day to

buy one unit of that mutual fund. That figure represents the total value of the stocks, bonds, et cetera, in the mutual's portfolio, divided by the number of units issued.

If you want to sell your mutual fund, your broker redeems your units at that day's posted price.

Some mutuals offer dividends. The cash dividend can be converted into more units within the mutual, or paid out directly to you.

Mutuals are just as varied as stocks in the types of investments they make. You can have mutuals that invest exclusively in mortgages or treasury bills, or stocks, or even gold. Some mutuals invest internationally, while others prefer to invest exclusively in Canada. There are general funds that invest in a little bit of everything, and there are balanced funds that are carefully designed by their managers to make sure the funds are not too dependent on any one financial investment.

Most funds charge a yearly administrative fee of between 1% to 2% of the value of the unit.

On top of that, there are commissions. In a "front-end load" your sales representative takes a cut, a percentage of the money you invest when you buy the mutual fund unit. When you go to sell, there is no selling charge.

In a "back-end loaded" mutual fund, you pay a fee when you sell the mutual fund. The longer the money is invested, the cheaper the back-end fee is to withdraw money out of the fund.

Finally, there's the "no-load" mutual fund, with no buying or selling commission. But nothing is free. No-load funds usually charge a slightly higher administrative fee, drawn from the funds' profits.

Picking a Mutual Fund

Once a month, most major financial newspapers publish mutual fund surveys. All mutual funds are listed, in percentage gain or loss, over the last 1, 3, 5 and 10 years.

Remember your investment pyramid. If you want security, then you'll want to invest in mutuals that specialize in interest-earning securities. If you want to shoot for the moon, then put an investment in your pyramid peak. There are mutuals that specialize in commodity purchases, or in the always gyrating precious metals market.

The safest mutual funds are those that buy mostly short-term government securities and treasury bills. They're called "money market" funds.

Income funds, funds that buy a mix of treasury bills, bonds, mortgages, or even preferred shares, are the next safest. These funds normally invest only in securities that earn a fixed rate of interest.

Mortgage funds invest only in mortgages. They are reasonably safe, as long as the fund is cautious about risk. Dividend-income funds make their money from investing in preferred shares that guarantee dividend returns every year. Blue-chip stock funds specialize in buying shares in solid, long-established companies.

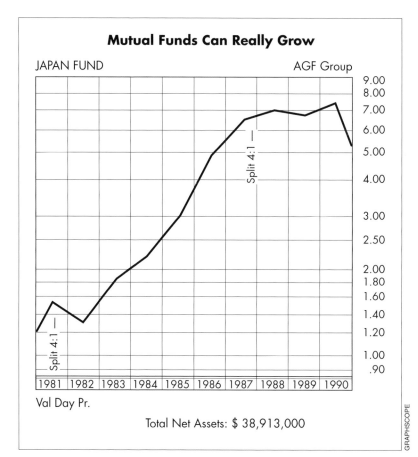

Higher-risk mutual funds include those that invest in foreign stocks and bonds, as well as foreign currencies. Real estate funds buy and sell real estate for their investors.

Growth funds are those specializing in selecting stocks investors think will dramatically rise in value.

Precious metal funds buy and sell gold and other precious metals. They're extremely risky, due to the unpredictability of precious metal prices.

At the very peak are options and commodity funds, funds that engage in highly speculative ventures.

Within any of the risk categories, the rules of analysis are the same:

Rule 1: Look for funds with the best long-term performance. A long-term record is a thumbnail sketch of how adaptable the fund managers have been. We've been through wild fluctuations in inflation, interest rates, currency, and commodity prices. Any fund that kept growing steadily through these economic storms had good hands at the helm.

Rule 2: Look for consistency: a continual, steady rate of growth of a mutual. Compare two funds that have averaged a 20% growth over the same time period. One might have grown in a volatile way, jumping 30% one year, crashing 20% the next, then soaring 50% the third year. The other might have averaged a steady 20% growth over the same period (remember, most funds have years where growth slows down). The intelligent conclusion must be that the steady growth fund will earn as good a return, with less risk. Over time, that mutual is likely to be a better bet than the periodic high flyer.

Open-Ended Mutual Funds

The "open-ended" mutual can expand or contract the number of units it has to offer on the market. If investors want to buy more units because they like the performance of a mutual, then all the mutual fund company has to do is issue more units at the going price. The units in an open-ended mutual fund reflect the actual value of the stocks they hold, every working day of the year.

If the fund sees a good investment opportunity, then it can raise capital by selling more units. The size of the "investment pool" in an open-ended mutual fund is continually changing.

Closed-End Mutual Funds

A "closed-end" mutual works on the same principle as an open-ended mutual fund. One company uses your money and the money of countless other investors to buy a large diversified portfolio of whatever financial investments they deem worthwhile.

The difference lies in how the shares are purchased or sold. A closed-end mutual behaves like a regular stock. It is listed on a public stock exchange, and can be sold person-to-person. (In the open mutual, only the fund buys back the units.) Only a limited number of shares in a closed-end mutual fund, not units, are issued. The number of shares remain fairly constant.

In the financial markets of the world, the closed-end shares are judged like any other share. Their value is determined by what the market will pay, not by the actual value of their assets. If you add up, and average, the posted value of all the stocks held in a closed-end mutual fund, you might find the mutual's actual value worked out to, say, $10 a share. But the market—buyers and sellers—might be trading the mutual's share at $7.

The advantage of a closed-end fund lies in the set number of shares. If the fund is doing well, then there's no dilution of profits. The share values are simply going to rise. In bull (good) markets, a closed-end fund usually rises to a higher price than an open-end fund holding the same investments.

Determining a sound closed-end mutual fund is the same as finding a sound open-ended mutual. Look for funds with a proven, consistent growth record. *Graphascope,* a book that tracks the long-term movement of closed-end funds in Canada, is available at some libraries and most brokerage firms. You'll find closed-end mutual performances tracked over 1- to 10-year periods.

Mutual Funds As an Investment

Mutual funds do make sense. You can pick and choose from among the world's best financial brains to decide who should invest your money for you. You do not need to labour over financial reports to check out which investments to invest in. That's the fund manager's job. Mutual fund managers can make investment decisions based on far more information than you could find.

By their diversity of investments, mutuals tend to be less volatile than individual stocks and are therefore a safer investment. For the small investor, for anybody with less than $50 000 to invest, a mutual fund allows you to indirectly diversify your holdings.

Open-ended mutuals are one of the few ways you can be forced to save by automatic monthly investments. There are funds that will take $50 a month to invest for you. There's no other way such small amounts can be directly invested in financial markets.

"Dollar cost averaging," as such monthly investing is called, means you are buying the mutual fund when it's high in price, and also buying at times when it's low. You "average out" your cost, which keeps you from making the mistake of buying in one shot at the top of the market.

Generally, the stock market has gone up in value. Buying into a mutual fund on a monthly basis will usually earn a good long-term return while greatly reducing your risk.

If trends from the past hold steady into the future, then mutual funds should earn a much better long-term rate of growth on your money than it would earn in a bank savings account. Then again, there's no guarantee. And that's why mutual funds should never be in the bottom level of your investment pyramid.

Turning Student Loans into a Nest Egg:
Jeremy Stuart

Jeremy Stuart is that fellow we all wish we had been. At 26, the first-year premed student has been buying mutual funds for eight years. Every year he takes out a student loan, for which he isn't charged interest. He invests it all, paying his tuition and living expenses from part-time jobs. Stuart has opted to invest in mutual funds as an indirect means of stock market investment. "I don't have the time to watch the market every day. Instead I try to find mutual fund managers with the best track records. I remember reading somewhere that $10 000 invested in the Templeton Growth Fund in 1953 would be worth $1.5 million today. I looked for mutual fund managers like that, people with extremely good long-term track records." Stuart has opted for the preauthorized chequing plan, or dollar-cost averaging. Every month, $200 is drawn from his bank account and invested into Templeton. "The last three years haven't been great for mutuals," Stuart said in 1991. "My patience has been tested. But don't forget, in the mid-1980s, Templeton was growing at the rate of 30% per year. I fully expect that as stocks get cheaper, Templeton will find some extremely good investment opportunities. Sooner or later, mutuals will come back to higher levels. Until then, I'll be patient." Stuart plans to keep investing, to buck up his investment rate once he's a doctor. He wants to have $2 million, and the option to retire, by the time he's 45.

The Stock Market

Once you know what you are doing, stock market investments have the potential to outperform most other investments for your retirement nest egg. In fact, in any five-year period since the turn of the century, stock investments have done better than

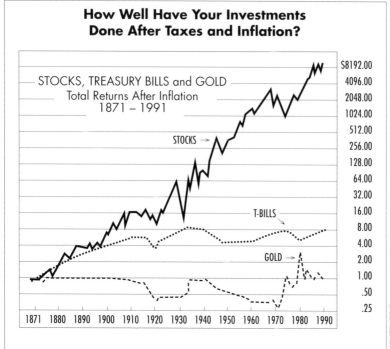

How Well Have Your Investments Done After Taxes and Inflation?

STOCKS, TREASURY BILLS and GOLD
Total Returns After Inflation
1871 – 1991

STOCKS →

T-BILLS

GOLD →

$8192.00
4096.00
2048.00
1024.00
512.00
256.00
128.00
64.00
32.00
16.00
8.00
4.00
2.00
1.00
.50
.25

1871 1880 1890 1900 1910 1920 1930 1940 1950 1960 1970 1980 1990

MARKET LOGIC

bank returns.

Common Shares

Shares represent ownership. Public companies, companies where stock is traded on public exchanges, issue shares to raise money. Those shares are bought and sold on the minute-to-minute determination of their value by investors. The whole idea of a common share (as opposed to a preferred share) is participation in a company's growth. The investor, by owning a chunk of a company, shares in its increasing assets and bottom-line profits. As the company grows, its shares go up in value. Small dividends, the annual payments made on a per-share basis (as determined by the company), can also sweeten the shareholder's pie.

The stock market is a psychological indicator. When investor confidence is high, stock markets tend to move up. When investors are pessimistic, stock markets tend to drop in price.

Stock markets predict future events. If investors think the economy will improve in the future, a "bull" market results, with most shares increasing in value. If investors believe the future economy looks grim, a "bear" market comes about, with most shares decreasing in value. Generally, stock markets move about six months in advance of future events. If investors feel a recession will soon be over, stocks generally begin to rise a half-year before the anticipated upswing. That's why, if you wait until a recession's over before you invest in the stock market, then you're usually too late.

In the short term, the strength of a company may have little relation to the value of its shares. In the long term, however, individual company performance is the key to good stock growth.

Blue-chip stocks

In the context of your financial pyramid, investing in stocks is no different from any other investment. Stocks do not belong in the foundation of your pyramid. But for the third floor of your pyramid, "blue-chip" stocks make sense.

"Blue chips" are the shares issued by proven companies, with long records of good management, steady earnings, and strong cash reserves.

Blue chips are unspectacular. They grow slowly, steadily, without fanfare, without roller coaster ups and downs in value.

Blue-chip stocks are among the least publicized, best ways to make the most of your money, without undertaking huge risk. If you invested in the 10 best blue-chip stocks in Canada, and then stuck the certificates in a trunk for 10 years, you would find those stocks would have earned you a better rate of return than any comparable "guaranteed" investment. Over the long term in modern financial markets, blue-chip stocks have always out-performed guaranteed investments.

Growth stocks

On the next level of your investment pyramid—a little more risk, a little more chance of bigger returns—are growth stocks.

Growth stocks are those issued by young, aggressive companies that have successfully marketed one or more products or services. These companies are doing well. Their shares have increased in value. But they are still a higher risk than blue chips, because they aren't as well established.

A good growth stock appreciates more quickly than blue-chip ones. Earnings aren't usually paid out in dividends, but instead are reinvested within the company.

A typical growth stock might be the Toronto Sun Publishing Company. In 1980, with three daily newspapers in Canada, its shares were worth $2. By 1988, the company had grown to five daily newspapers, and many weeklies, magazines, and printing operations. Through several bull and bear markets, TorSun share value had grown to a peak of $28 a share.

Growth stocks can also plummet. With the stock market in the doldrums of late 1991, TorSun shares had shrunk to $14 a share. By late 1992, TorSun was in the $16-$17 range.

Penny stocks

Then there's the top of your investment pyramid: the hot tips, the sure winners, the big gamble.

They are called penny stocks—shares issued in new, unproven companies with no past track records. Penny shares are wildly speculative. They can be a huge success or a crashing failure.

Junior mining companies issue lots of penny stock. You

might buy a penny mining stock in the hope it will be the one company to hit a huge gold-bearing mineral deposit.

If you can't afford to lose your money and walk away unconcerned, then you shouldn't be investing in penny stocks.

Treat penny stocks like a day at the races. They're just as speculative, and just as entertaining. But if your penny stock hits the jackpot, get your dollars out fast! Transfer your profits down to safer levels of your pyramid.

Never, ever let your pyramid get distorted. Many people walk the streets who made a killing, got greedy, and put their profits back into more penny stocks, until they had no more money.

Preparing to Invest

As a conservative investor, you can probably do very well in the stock market if you only invest in sound companies, and buy and sell shares at the right times.

Patience is the key. Learn to crawl before you walk, walk before you run. Study the stock market for years before you invest a cent. You've got your lifetime to invest. You shouldn't put substantial amounts of money into the stock market before you've paid off your mortgage, or before a strong foundation in income-producing investments has been established within your pyramid.

Begin by visiting three or four reputable brokers. These people will see you as a potential long-term client. (See Chapter 12 on choosing your financial team.) Ask each one to recommend several blue-chip, growth, and penny stocks for you to watch … but not invest in as yet.

Take your time. Learn the language. Read the financial pages of the newspapers. Read the reams of company and "sector" information published by brokerage firms and research houses. Watch the performance of your targeted companies over a couple of years. Every stock has its ups and downs. Over time, you'll recognize the trading patterns of your particular stocks—when they are up in value, when they are down.

If you take that time, studying the market while you are investing every excess dime in paying off your mortgage, you will learn to overcome the biggest obstacle to successful stock market investing: your own fear and greed. You'll learn to laugh at the "Chicken Little" (the sky is falling!) syndrome—the panic to sell a stock and lose money when the stock is dropping in value. If you have properly trained yourself, you'll buy into companies you've been following for years when that stock is at the low end of a cycle. Then you'll hang on to the stock for a very long time.

Unless you're profit taking for a particular reason, there's no point in selling a good stock until the later stages of your life when you're gradually converting your riskier ventures into interest-earning investments for a secure retirement. Buy quality stocks. Buy cheap, and keep adding to your stock inventory when prices drop back. Over the long haul, you'll do very well.

Resist "quick fixes," fear, and greed. Historically, the return on reputable stocks listed in Canada has been significantly higher than the guaranteed rates of return on bonds, debentures, savings bonds, and savings accounts.

Cautious, knowledgeable adventures in the stock market may prove to be some of the best investments you can make in the growth section of your pyramid.

Golden Rules of Stock Market Investing

1. Buy reputable stocks within the boundaries of your own financial pyramid. Don't get carried away and over-invest in a risky investment. Don't upset the balance of your all-important pyramid.
2. Buy quality stocks when they're cheap. When the rats are deserting the ship, that's usually the best time to crawl back on … as long as you know the hull is sound.
3. When those stocks drop again, buy some more. Take advantage of dips in the market to increase your holdings in a good company.
4. Diversify: As time goes by, try to purchase shares in companies that operate in different parts of the economy. This is a means to buffer yourself against wild fluctuations in some businesses. Your oil company stock might plummet because the Arabs have decided to flood the crude oil

market. But your airline stock may be having a banner year, thanks to cheap fuel costs. They balance each other. And it might be a great time to buy more oil stock.

5. Keep your cool. Never panic when markets drop. They always go up and down. Over the long haul, they have historically seen their value increase steadily upward. Look at times of panic selling as golden investment opportunities.

6. There are brokers out there who specialize in the "buy, sell, churn and burn" school of investing. They are more concerned with their commissions than your financial well-being. Avoid them.

7. Hang on to what you have. Don't sell your quality stocks, except when somebody makes you an offer you can't refuse. A good stock, through its peaks and valleys, will keep getting better. Eventually, you'll cash in the stock at one of its peaks.

8. Have fun with the tip of your pyramid. Throw a little cash at a "hot" stock, just to see what happens.

Investing Is Fun:
Joyce Richards

At 75, Joyce Richards could sell her half-million dollar stock portfolio, put everything into government-backed bonds, and never again check a stock market price. But why should she? "Investing is too much fun," the retired teacher says. "I get a thrill out of buying when everybody else is selling, and selling when others are buying."

Richards was a comparative latecomer to the stock market. Her husband died in 1956, leaving her at the age of 34 with two kids, $5000 cash, a house worth $13 000 and a 10-year mortgage. "I wanted to invest some money, but all I could afford in the 1950s was about $10 a month. By the 1970s, I was up to about $200 a month. Now I live on my pension, and put about $25 000 a year from dividend payments back into my investments. "I'm a fairly simple person. I just didn't feel good about investing in government bonds. Companies are motivated to make money, but governments are motivated to spend it."

Joyce's investment strategy was straightforward. She bought

stocks in stable industries, rarely sold those stocks, and reinvested the dividends.

"I have always looked for companies with low debt that paid a high yearly dividend to stockholders. I figured anybody who could afford to pay out cash had to be making money. None of the major banks in this country have ever gone bankrupt. Utilities have their profits legislated by government. Pipelines are necessary because everybody has to heat their homes. Phone companies are good investments. People are always going to use their phones."

As major companies issued new stock in the 1960s, Joyce bought in, a few shares at a time. She bought new stock offered by TD Bank, Alberta Energy, Bell, and TransCanada Pipelines. Many of Joyce's stocks today pay an annual dividend many times greater than what she originally paid for the stock. The only time she sells stock, she says, is when the price becomes "unrealistically high. But in most cases, the stocks I hold are slow and steady." Her age, Joyce says, may be a major advantage. She's been through at least seven bad stock markets. In 1987, markets dropped by 30%, 25% in 1982, 40% in 1974 … not to mention major market drops in the 1950s and 1960s.

"One thing always struck me. The price of shares always went back up again, to higher levels than they'd ever been before. I learned early on that you have to buy when nobody else wants to. The lower a stock goes, the more upside potential it has. In 1987, when people were panic-stricken by the crash, I was phoning my broker. It was the finest time possible to be buying more stock."

Real Estate

A rental property can be a terrific investment, if you are well informed on your current real estate market, and know an extremely good buy when you see one. You must also be content in your home town, and plan to stay put for the long term. Nothing is worse than trying to manage properties by long-distance telephone. You must have enough extra monthly income to subsidize the property, if necessary, through a few lean years when rental income drops.

Purchasing residential homes for rental purposes has some

enormous investment attractions.

1. Unlike almost any other kind of investment, you borrow most of the money (the mortgage), and then have somebody else (the tenant) meet the payments.
2. Despite cyclical ups and downs, real estate generally increases in value over the years. It should at least keep up with inflation, and can, depending on when and where you are investing in Canada, reap windfall profits.
3. Taking a mortgage out on a rental property is, in effect, a forced savings plan. No matter how the market price goes up and down, equity is built up in the property with each payment. It's much better than saving nothing, as often happens when you are not forced to save.
4. You're unlikely to pay much income tax, if any, on your rental property income. The mortgage interest payments, repairs, and improvements are deductions against rental income.
5. If you bought a rental property before March 1992, part of the increase in value when you go to sell could be regarded as a capital gain by Revenue Canada. Your profit could be subject to certain tax exemptions, depending on your financial situation.
6. As your first rental property is paid off, you can set up an investment cycle, borrowing more money against your original investment property to use as a down payment on another house.

Sweat Equity:
John Smith

John Smith in Calgary was smart enough to be reasonably well set up—as a small-time conservative investor—when oil prices crashed in the early 1980s. Houses that were selling for $100 000 dropped to $70 000. He bought a house for $70 000: $20 000 down, $50 000 in a mortgage. On average, the mortgage cost him $500 a month over a 25-year period, taxes were about $140 a month, and maintenance another $100 a month. His costs totalled $740 a month. At first, he could only get $600 a month rental for the house, since the market was slack. The rental property was costing him $140 a month out of pocket. That was tolerable. He had a secure job with seniority. His own home, almost paid off, wasn't too expensive to maintain. Two years later, the rental market began to recover. Income began to catch up with expenditures. The rental house started to pay its own way. Ten years later, Calgary began to boom again. John put his rental property up for sale. The house was sold for $110 000. Meanwhile, the mortgage had been reduced to $40 000. Even with $10 000 deducted to pay the lawyers, real estate agents, and appraisers, John turned his original investment of $20 000 (plus $3500 in initial subsidization) into $56 500.

John had invested a lot of "sweat equity" into the house, but that's a healthy tax-free return on his original investment. John could have been caught on the risky side of investing in real estate. He could have bought during the oil boom when house prices were at their highest. He could have paid as low a down payment as possible, and taken a large mortgage. He could very easily have been forced to sell, like so many small investors, when real estate prices collapsed. Had his timing been wrong, John would have gone bankrupt.

Buying raw land—land with no buildings—is a speculative investment. If the price stays stagnant, then you are faced with the fact there is no rental income coming in. Property taxes still have to be paid, mortgage payments still have to be met.

There's another possibility, as your financial smarts improve.

Owning apartments can be profitable, if you can afford to purchase them. A good apartment building can usually weather a recession. If the rental vacancy is 30%, a 100-unit building should still have 70 units occupied, producing a cash flow. Duplexes, or any home with suites built in, have the practical advantage of keeping you, as the landlord, right on top of your tenant.

Golden Rules of Real Estate

1. Make sure you're financially stable before you start. Keep any real-estate investing in the third level of your financial pyramid.
2. Timing is everything. Never buy real estate at the peak of the market. In fact, buy real estate when nobody else wants it.
3. Make sure you have enough cash reserves to cover rental

property emergencies.
4. Be ultra-cautious in your financial projections. Assume you are making a long-term investment.
5. Make sure you're buying the best possible house, at the cheapest price, in the best area you can afford. Rentability and resale value is everything.

The Handy Millionaire:
Brenda White

Three years ago, 57-year-old Brenda White decided to retire from the beverage company where she'd spent most of her career as a customer service representative. She did, after all, own 12 houses, mortgage-free. You'd never know it to look at her—Brenda prefers jeans to dresses, and has no use for the high life—but she's easily worth $1.5 million.

Brenda never set out to become wealthy. A farm girl, she moved into the city in 1960, and with her new husband bought a basic bungalow home for $14 000. That was a fair chunk of cash, and with a first mortgage costing $85 per month and a second at $25, it was a tough haul for the first few years. The smartest thing she did, Brenda says, was to buy a house that had a basement suite. "We always saved the rent from the suite. By 1965, we had a little cash in the bank, and I decided to buy a second house. Mortgage rates were around 5%, and I couldn't think of anything else to invest in that was as practical as another house."

It was hardly a complicated approach to the process of accumulating wealth. "Every time there was a little cash in the bank account, we'd buy another house. By the third one, in 1967, I started to figure out there were actually some tax advantages." The houses basically paid for themselves from rental income, Brenda says, "though occasionally we used money from our wages to cut down mortgages." She just kept buying: a fourth house in 1967, a fifth in 1971, a sixth in 1973. By 1978, she had all 12. "I never really bothered with the accounting end," says Brenda. "It took me 10 years before I added up the numbers. That was a nice surprise."

Brenda's dislike of large mortgages was her saving grace. By the late 1970s in Alberta, she decided to stop buying, since houses, she thought, were becoming too expensive. The rental income beyond the regular expenses of maintenance, taxes, and mortgage payments went towards a full-scale attack on those mortgages. By 1982, when the Alberta economy went into a tailspin, Brenda was debt-free.

Brenda had one big advantage which all individuals seeking conservatively acquired, independent financial security require. She wasn't afraid to work hard. She never begrudged the additional workload that running 12 houses required. "I enjoy maintaining them," she says. "I'm reasonably handy. Overall, I'd say I didn't spend more than four hours a week on the houses."

Her only regret is that she didn't get into a few small apartment blocks earlier in the game. "I wish I'd started sooner," she says. "And maybe I should have looked for more advice sooner … but then again, I might have been steered in the wrong direction!"

Rolling the Dice— High Risk, High Reward

*There are two times in a man's life when he should
not speculate. When he can afford it, and when he can't.*
—Mark Twain

The tip of your pyramid is saved for small, high-risk investments. They might pay off spectacularly, or they might be dust in the wind. This chapter is on investing for fun, that 5%-10% of your investment for the future that you can afford to lose without ulcers, thoughts of suicide, or other forms of personal financial pandemonium.

Gold

The Midas Touch, the gold standard, the Klondike gold rush ... through the centuries, gold has been viewed as the global "storehouse of value."

Gold is hard to find, hard to produce. If all the gold ever produced on this planet were collected and dumped into one big pile, it would measure 16.5 metres wide, 16.5 metres long, and 16.5 metres high ... in other words, about the size of a small warehouse.

Gold is considered the ultimate protection against all kinds of economic calamity—inflation, depression, war, famine. When other forms of value have no security, gold has historically maintained its value.

Gold: You can feel it, taste it, bang your head against it. Unlike most other investments, it's physically real.

Gold prices usually move in reaction to the global economy. When the economy is strong, when inflation is low, and when the American dollar is strong, investors tend to sell their gold, and it falls in price. When economies are shaky, when people are fearful about their investments, they often start buying gold. Its price will rise.

Until 1972, the price of gold was "fixed" by the United States at $35 an ounce. But in that year, the American government realized it could no longer afford to buy enough gold to keep converting American dollars to gold at that rate. The "gold standard" was dropped. Gold was left to find its own value against the currencies of the world.

In countries where the political and economic conditions are turbulent, gold is a fundamental means of saving. The value of all currencies, including the Canadian dollar, depends on the confidence world traders have in the country's economy. Whatever the world thinks your country is worth, so shall your dollar, yen, or peso rise and fall compared to other currencies.

Gold transcends national currencies. It has universal value. If Canada were experiencing runaway inflation, the value of our currency would fall internationally. Canadians would begin buying gold to protect themselves against the lesser value of our dollar.

If you had to move to another part of the world in a hurry, gold is one of the most universally accepted methods of carrying your assets with you ... especially in countries with currencies that are near-worthless on international markets. In that way, gold could be viewed as the most conservative of investments. Indeed, many Canadians do buy small quantities of gold and store it themselves ... just in case, they say, the country falls apart.

The actual price of gold dramatically rises and falls in value, according to supply and demand. If there's fear, then gold is sought, and its value rises. A stable investment climate makes gold drop in value.

Gold isn't an income-producing investment. It just sits there. In 1987, for instance, an ounce of gold traded in the $350 to $400 range. By December 1992, it was still in that same price range.

Buying gold to make money follows the same formula as any other investment. One hopes to buy gold at a low point in its value cycle. And one plans to sell at a peak, when the rest of the world wants to hop on the same bandwagon. Gold prices, after all, are motivated primarily by supply and demand.

Buying and Selling Gold

Most of us think of gold in terms of gold bars, or gold wafers. The actual purchasing of the metal itself is but one of many ways to invest in gold. There are gold coins, gold jewelry, gold certificates, gold stocks, gold mutual funds, even gold options and futures.

Gold Bullion

You can walk into any major bank, usually its regional headquarters, and actually buy gold, in weights from 5 grams (about the size of a pencil eraser) to gold bars of 500 troy ounces (about 40 pounds).

Gold varies in its level of purity, from 0.995 to 0.9999% pure gold. The purity will affect the price of the gold you are buying.

Always buy gold made by reputable refiners, and that bears the producer's stamp. The Royal Canadian Mint is internationally recognized as a reputable producer of gold. In private companies, Engelhard Industries, or Johnson and Matthey Ltd., are respected names.

The advantage of buying gold bullion is that it can be sold anywhere, at any time, for any currency in the world. No other investment—apart from the American dollar—is so quickly, and so universally, convertible to cash. And if the world looks as if it is heading towards economic ruin, a quick return can be earned on gold.

The disadvantages are the additional costs associated with the buying, selling, and storing of gold bullion. Service charges can knock the value out of a gold bullion investment. The seller always maintains a small profit over the quoted gold price of the day. There's a "bar charge" depending on the size of the bar, a "pouring charge," and a sales tax in most Canadian provinces on the purchase of gold bullion. You wouldn't want to leave your gold bullion on the mantel at home. There are storage charges to think of, either in your safety deposit box, or in a vault. When you go to sell your gold, there are weighing, or "assaying" charges. Institutions often charge a "buying" fee to purchase your gold.

Gold Coins

Gold coins often prove to be a profitable investment. The actual gold value of the coin—almost always a troy ounce (a system of measurement with 12 troy ounces to the pound) can be enhanced by the potential "numismatic," or collectable value, of the coin.

The expertise in coin collecting comes from knowing which coins will increase in value, and which ones won't. The numismatic premium can vary from 10% to 200% or more over the actual value of the gold in the coin. In the mid-1980s, the Chinese issued a gold "Panda" coin that dramatically increased in value due to a small supply and great demand.

Gold coins are issued by many countries. The coins can be bought and sold through major banks. In Canada we have the Maple Leaf gold coin, the Australians have the Gold Nugget coin, the Americans their American Eagle, the South Africans have the Krugerrand. The Japanese have the Hirohito coin, named after the Japanese emperor.

A gold coin is more expensive to buy than actual bullion. Often a sales tax is charged.

If you buy a coin that has numismatic value, you can possibly earn a better future return than you could with bullion. But don't scratch the coin! Any blemish on a gold coin causes a major drop in its collectable value.

Gold Jewelry

Gold jewelry is usually seen as a visual delight rather than a financial investment. Gold jewelry can be melted down strictly for its gold value, but don't kid yourself. Much of the cost of gold jewelry lies in its design and creation. It may have collectable value if the jewelry has historical or artistic merit. If jewelry was melted down to its bullion form, you would never retrieve the cost of the jewelry from the bullion alone. Don't count on making money from your jewelry. Second-hand jewelry usually sells for 25 cents on the dollar.

Pure gold is too soft for jewellers to work with properly, and so it is usually mixed with nickel, copper, silver, zinc (for hardness) or other alloys (for colour). Mixed with copper, gold is orange. With silver, it's "white" gold. Twenty-four karat means the gold in the jewelry is 100% pure. Eighteen karat is 75% gold. Fourteen karat is 58% gold, and ten karat, the legal minimum for gold jewelry in North America, is 42% gold.

Gold Certificates

Gold certificates are cheaper than gold bullion or gold coins to buy. They cost less to store, and are almost as easy to convert into cash as gold bullion.

Gold certificates are issued by certain banks and trust companies. You buy a certificate, at today's prices, and you are given the "right"—if you want to exercise it—to take delivery of the gold you have purchased at any future time.

As long as you are certain the institution guarantees that the gold is locked away in a vault, this is probably the most practical way to purchase gold.

There are buying and selling fees, but at about 2% per transaction, they're cheaper than the actual buying and selling of bullion and coins. You avoid storage fees. If you redeem your certificate for cash, there won't be a sales tax. And you can place the certificate in an account with a broker. Then again, you wouldn't have the fun of holding, touching, and hoarding the real thing.

Investing in Gold Mines or Gold Stocks

Investing in gold mines, even the most well-established, is always a gamble. Investing in a junior gold mine stock is about as speculative as you can get. More often than not, gold mining companies don't make money. But they are a popular investment, because the "big hit" can make gold stock prices soar. Gold mining is at the mercy of nature and world markets for gold. Depending on the quality of the gold ore, the price of production can vary from $150 to $300 an ounce. If the world market for gold collapses, as it has done from time to time in recent history, then the mine you have invested in is unlikely to sell its gold profitably. It will probably shut down. If gold prices soar, and the mine you have invested in is an efficient producer, then the stock can leap in value.

Gold mine stocks can be placed in an RRSP. There's no tax on buying a gold stock, and it can be cheaper than buying gold itself.

Gold stocks can fly like eagles, or crash like crippled airplanes, depending on the price of gold on world markets, and depending on the ability of the company to extract gold from the ore competitively.

Gold Mutuals

Gold mutual funds specialize in the buying and selling of gold bullion, gold stocks, coins, and just about anything to do with gold. It has all the advantages of any mutual. You entrust your gold investing to a professional manager, who is an expert in all things to do with gold. In turn, the mutual will charge a management fee, and you will pay a broker a commission to get your money in and out of the gold mutual fund. The disadvantages are like any gold-related investment. The risk may be less than investing in a gold stock, or gold bullion. It's still one of the more speculative investments around.

Gold Options and Futures

Options and futures are ways in which a small amount of cash gives you the right to buy or sell large amounts of gold at a set price for a specific period of time.

Gold options and futures are very leveraged (only a small down payment is required) and very, very risky—like buying a $1 million house with a $10 000 down payment, but still being responsible for the balance of the mortgage if the real estate value goes down.

Other Precious Metals

Other precious metals behave in a similar fashion to gold, and can be bought and sold through similar techniques.

Silver is called "the poor man's gold." It's not so much a precious metal any more as an industrial metal. Today, the price of silver is determined by its supply and demand for industrial use, like copper or zinc.

Platinum and palladium, rare metals used for high-technology manufacturing, are also high-risk investments. Because they are produced in minute quantities, and are viewed as insurance against inflation or economic collapse, their value moves in line with gold prices.

As a rule of thumb, 5% of a diversified investment portfolio may be placed in precious metal investments as a safeguard against inflation. But never let precious metals, or any other high-risk investment, expand beyond the tip of your own financial pyramid.

Other High-Risk Investments

Junior/Penny Stocks

The name describes them well: Junior, or penny, stocks are like any other common stocks. They're just more risky. Be it a gold claim or a basement invention, there are always businesspeople with a big idea, but no money. The stock market, through junior stocks, is an avenue where they can raise what's known as "venture capital."

The small long-shot stock can be a winner. Once upon a time a tiny computer company called Apple went to the stock market looking to raise venture capital—the rest is history. But the odds are heavily against the new company. Like new restaurants, 80% to 90% of high-risk venture investments fail.

Your best bet, at least to give the odds a better chance, is information. Be aware of what you are buying, what the offering is, what the potential product is. Unless you are personally familiar with the product on offer, you're better off steering clear of a long shot.

The reputation of the promoter is important. Junior stock salespeople often have little regard for your interests. They may be attempting to bring the price of a junior stock up, creating demand by means of a well-rehearsed sales pitch. Then, by being negative at the right time, the promoter may cause a selling spree that sends the stock down in price. Unscrupulous promoters can work the up-and down-action to their own advantage. They can bring the price down so they can personally buy. They can push the price up, so they can personally sell. Never rely on the promoter's pitch. Find out what the professionals think of the investment. Does it have any merit? Does it have a shot at success? Investigate the players. Does the manager, the entrepreneur, have a good reputation? Have they put their own money into the venture, have they remortgaged their homes in order to get their product off the ground? Or are the main players in the junior stock issue strictly there for the quick buck?

On the exchanges where the "juniors" trade, like Vancouver or Alberta, firms are not as regulated as in more formal exchanges. The selfish sharpie can sometimes manipulate junior stocks, without being slapped on the wrist.

Timing is important in buying a junior stock. Often a new "penny" stock, beginning at five cents, will quickly double or triple in value based on sheer speculation. And then, just as quickly, fall back.

If you've received a hot tip from your third cousin, it's likely the rest of the planet is already on to it. If the penny stock has jumped considerably in value, be careful. Having doubled or tripled, it's more than likely to drop. If you bought at 5 cents and can sell at 15 cents, you should. Fast.

Golden Rules of Junior Stock Investing
1. Do your homework. Know what you're getting into.
2. Invest only the tip of your financial pyramid.
3. Buy before anybody else decides to buy.
4. Sell before everyone else decides to sell.

Selling Short

Because large institutional stockholders, like brokerage firms, are willing to lend out stock, money can be made when stocks drop dramatically in value.

The technique is called short-selling. Here's how it works: You have a well-informed hunch that the value of a stock is about to plunge in price. You go to your broker and borrow stock in that company from the brokerage firm. You are expected to return the same number of shares sometime in the future. You then immediately sell the borrowed stock.

If the stock drops in value, then you will profit. You buy the stock back—to return to the brokerage firm—at a lower price than you sold it. For example, the price of a stock is $10. You borrow the stock and then immediately sell it, pocketing $10. When the time comes to return the stock to the institution you borrowed it from, its value has dropped to $5. You buy it back at $5. You wind up with a $5 profit, minus commissions.

Selling short is one of the stock market's riskiest games. If the stock does not drop, but instead rises dramatically, you're in deep trouble. Say you sell the borrowed stock for $10. This time, the price rises to $30. You must buy the same number of shares that were lent to you in the first place. You've lost $20 a share.

Warrants and Rights

Warrants are "privileges" that come as an accessory when a company sells new stock. It's an incentive to encourage you to buy that stock.

Warrants are issued with the stock. They allow the buyer to pick up more of the same shares, for a specified period of time, at a preset price.

If the stock goes up, then the warrant (the right to buy the stock at the predetermined price) also increases in value. If the stock drops to less than its original price, then the warrant holder might as well tear up the warrant. It's worthless.

Warrants act like a mini-stock on their own. They're frequently bought and sold, independently of the stock they were issued with, before they expire. Say a stock rises from $10 to $15 a share, a 50% rise in value. The warrant giving the right to buy at $10 was originally trading at $1. Now that the stock has gone up by $5, the warrant will normally rise by at least $5 in value. While the stock has gone up by 50%, the warrant has appreciated by 500%. But if the stock drops below $10, the warrant quickly loses value.

The attraction of warrants is the lack of capital outlay. You need to invest only a small amount of money to ride on top of a successful stock.

Warrants are a stock accessory, like air-conditioning in cars. If the company needs to raise money in a bad market, the warrant is an additional incentive, a way to sweeten the pie.

Warrants can be highly speculative. But if the stock is successful, then a small investment in its warrants can yield a higher profit than actually buying the stock itself. On the other hand, if the stock doesn't go up in value before the warrant expires, then the warrant is not worth the paper it is printed on.

Rights are similar to warrants, but they expire sooner, and are only issued to existing shareholders, not as part of a new share issue. The "right" is the "right" to buy more stock, at levels slightly below the existing market price. Rights normally expire within a couple of months. Within their limited shelf-life, rights can also be bought and sold on the stock market. Like warrants, rights are issued by a company as an incentive for stockholders to purchase more stock.

Options

Put in their simplest form (they can get immensely complicated), options are bets—legally placed bets—that a particular stock, bond, or commodity will quickly appreciate or depreciate in value. Options are best left to experts. They can be highly speculative. You require a great deal of market knowledge and impeccable timing.

In a "call" option, the optimist bets the stock or commodity is going to rise in value. You pay a fee to the holder of the stock or commodity for the option to buy the stock or commodity at a set price in the future. If the stock or commodity goes up, the call-option buyer (you) will make money. But if it goes down, you lose.

In a "put" option, the pessimist bets a stock or commodity will drop in value. If you're right, the put-option buyer (you) profit. If you're wrong, you lose your option fee.

Commodity Futures

Commodities are physical things, like grain, lumber, pork bellies (bacon), orange juice, or soybeans. The investor takes a contract, an undertaking to buy and receive a certain amount of a commodity, or sell and deliver the same commodity at a fixed price at a future fixed date.

Farmers and companies use commodity futures for practical reasons. It's a way farmers can guarantee a market price for their grain in six months' time. It's a way a brewery can ensure its barley supply for a year, at a known cost … no matter what happens to the price in the interim.

For the gambler, commodities are a high-risk game. When you buy or sell a futures contract, you're obliged to actually receive or deliver those goods on a specified day. The only way you can get out of physical delivery is by unloading the contract—at a profit or a loss—to somebody else.

A futures contract can be acquired by putting up only 5% of the contract value. But if you bet wrong, you're on the hook for the total amount of what you have promised. Say you enter a contract. You promise to deliver 20 000 bushels of wheat in five months, at $2 a bushel. You haven't seen the wheat and don't know where it will come from. But you have locked yourself into selling that wheat for $40 000 in five months. You have paid $2000 for the right to "control" that wheat at that price. But a drought hits the prairies. Prices soar. By the time you must deliver the wheat, as per your contract, you have to buy the actual wheat for $80 000.

You never see the wheat but your $2000 investment has turned into a $40 000 loss. The brokerage firm, which put up the other 95% of the price, can now demand you come up with the $38 000 cash to cover the loss.

Commodities are dangerous, like buying that $1 million house with $5000 down. It doesn't matter if real estate prices drop terribly. The purchaser is responsible for paying the rest of the $995 000. Commodity futures are for the very experienced investor, or for those adventurous sorts who have a built-in death wish. Until you can afford to lose, say, about $10 000 from the tip of your financial pyramid, steer clear of commodity futures.

A Hot Little Gold Mine:
Joe Valenti

Joe Valenti *was* a contented man. A business he had started out of his basement 35 years earlier, making gold chains and rings, had multiplied into a chain of five jewellery stores. Valenti had a net worth of over $1 million.

At a wedding one fateful June weekend, Joe's friend Luigi pulled him aside. Luigi had put his life's savings—$30 000— into a gold mine stock on the Vancouver Stock Exchange. The company had discovered unbelievable reserves of gold on its property. Luigi had originally bought at 60 cents a share. By the time of the wedding, the stock had already doubled. Luigi wanted to borrow some money from Joe to buy more. Joe was curious. He lent Luigi some money. Sure enough, in 90 days, the stock had doubled again, to $2.40 a share. Luigi was absolutely certain the stock would be at $30 by the year's end. They could both be rich beyond their wildest dreams.

Joe couldn't resist the lure of the hot gold-mine penny stock. He invested $100 000 at $2.50. Sure enough, the little stock that grew kept growing, to $6 almost overnight. Joe was in awe. His $100 000 had turned into $250 000 in less than two weeks. Joe went to the bank and withdrew $500 000. Half he lent to Luigi, the other half he used to buy stock for himself, at $6 a share. The stock still went up ... another 30 cents.

Then things started going awry. The ore deposits were not quite as rich as originally anticipated. The stock dropped back to $4. But Joe had faith. He put in another $100 000. Another annoying problem came up. The processing mill at the mine site was only able to produce half as much gold per day as had been projected. The stock sank to $3. Then gold prices began to drop. Dramatically. The company made a public declaration that it was in bad shape. But the problems were short term. Most investors weren't listening, and the price fell back to $1. Joe had faith. The stock was a bargain. He took his last $100 000 in readily available cash, and bought more shares at $1 each. The problems, after all, were short term. Indeed they were. Four days later, the stock closed at 22 cents. Luigi was fearful for his life. He'd borrowed $750 000 from all kinds of people. He committed himself to a mental hospital.

Joe, who'd built a business from scratch to having $1 million in cash, had now parlayed that million into $50 000.

Avoiding the Taxman

*And I beheld, and lo, a black horse; and he that sat
on him had a pair of balances in his hand.*

—Revelation 6:5

In spite of what the government is saying about cutting back on
spending, and lowering taxes—the bottom line is that modern
government is spending more every year than it takes in. Government is in a life and death struggle to pay for thousands of
programs. You are being taxed to death: GST, federal income
tax, provincial income tax, property tax, sales taxes, road taxes,
utility taxes, improvement surcharge taxes, and so on. Experts

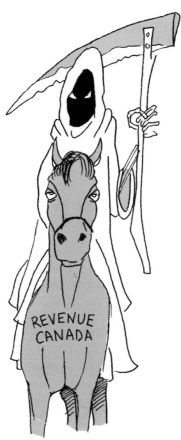

have calculated that you, as a middle-income salaried person, are doing nothing with your salary for the first six months of the year but paying taxes. Welcome to July! You can finally keep what you earn.

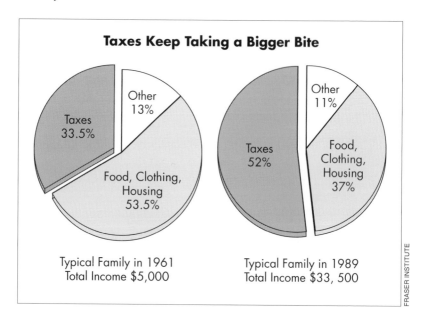

Taxes Keep Taking a Bigger Bite

Taxes 33.5%
Other 13%
Food, Clothing, Housing 53.5%

Typical Family in 1961
Total Income $5,000

Taxes 52%
Other 11%
Food, Clothing, Housing 37%

Typical Family in 1989
Total Income $33, 500

FRASER INSTITUTE

It's your money. You have the right to use every possible legal tax-break to keep your money. You have to think of the taxman as your mortal enemy. He's a highwayman in a black mask and cape, waiting to rob you on your way home from work, every day. Almost half your income! So much of it is sneaky tax—gasoline tax, booze tax, and other indirect taxes.

The taxman is not a bogeyman when you're 20 or 30 years old. Thanks to RRSPs, you can salt away a good chunk of your income in the early stages of your life, planning for your post-55 years. He's the Devil, when you're in your mid-30s or later, your house is paid off, and you want to put away more income than is allowable in your RRSP. Should your hard work and intelligence push you up towards the top of the salary scale, for every dollar you earn over $55 000, the taxman will demand almost *half* for the government's insatiable appetite.

Let's be blunt. As you approach $40 000 a year of net taxable income, you have to start protecting yourself against the taxman. If you don't find ways to reduce your taxable income at that point, you'll be a financial casualty. Taxation, coupled with inflation, will put you in a slow, subtle, net-loss position.

You must find an accountant who hates paying taxes as much as you do. You want one who will give you advice and who has initiative. Accounting is an art, not a science. An excellent accountant will take you to the edge of the cliff, but not over. A good accountant should have the creative flair to build your case, to help you reduce your taxes. A bad accountant won't take you within five kilometres of the financial edge. A good accountant will take you to five millimetres of that edge in order to claim everything possible on your behalf. The account- ant knows that, on the other side, the taxman is after your bucks. A good tax advisor, which is what an accountant is, is not a boastful frill but a necessity. If you retire with a healthy bank account, then your aggressive accountant is your best friend.

Tax avoidance is based on information, what you can or cannot do, what investments the government has ordained to be less severely taxed than others. Tax avoidance is a game of percentage points. It can be very confusing. But when your RRSP is as big as it can be, when you've paid off your house and have more investment cash, when you jump into the

How Investments are Taxed

1990 Effective Tax Rate Chart
(Based on a 53% Provincial Tax Rate)

Taxable Income Bracket	Interest	Capital Gains	Canadian Dividends
$0-28,275	26.9%	20.2%	7.2%
28,276-56,550	41.1	30.8	25.0
56,551-69,967	45.8	34.4	30.9
69,968 & over	46.7	35.0	31.5

CANADIAN PERSONAL TAX PLANNING GUIDE BY MARWICK THORN

$55 000-plus bracket at work, you'll want to know just as much as you can.

Here, for instance, is one bit of tax information that could save you thousands of dollars a year. If you have treasury bills, Canada Savings Bonds, or guaranteed investment certificates outside of your RRSP, the money they earn will be fully taxable. But if you have blue-chip stocks that traditionally pay a healthy dividend, those dividends are taxed at a much lower rate than interest-earning investments.

You have to look at investments where you can earn a decent buck, without giving most of it away to the taxman.

A "capital gain"—the profit you earn when you sell certain assets at a better price than you bought them for—gets a big break from the taxman.

The first $100 000 you make in capital gains (with a few exceptions) is tax-free.

When you do top that $100 000 mark, the game of percentage points sets in. Only 75% of your capital gain, not the full amount, is taxed.

Capital Gains:
Jane Doe

Jane Doe, outside her RRSP investments, has just cashed in a stock that performed extremely well for her. She's made a capital gain of $10 000. She has, however, already used up her $100 000 capital gain tax exemption. Her capital-gain profit of $10 000, however, will only be taxed as if it were $7500. She'll have to give over half of $7500 to the taxman, because she's now making over $55 000 a year. So she winds up paying $3750 from her $10 000 profit to the taxman. If it had been a $10 000 profit from a bond, or any other interest-earning investment, she'd be forced to hand over $5000 to the taxman. Interest income is fully taxed.

This book stresses conservative, restrained investment. And here we are telling you (as you cross the $55 000 sonic tax barrier into the 50% tax bracket) to go into riskier forms of investment, because of the tax savings. This appears to be a contradiction. In fact, there is no contradiction. You would never, ever, upset your financial pyramid. But you might fill your RRSP with interest-earning investments that otherwise would be taxed at full taxable value. Your dividend and capital-gains investments might then be left outside the RRSP, because the government would not take such a big bite of your profit. As a rule of thumb, those fully taxable investments should go into your RRSP.

Armed with the current tax laws, your aggressive account-ant can advise you, given your age and financial circumstances, on which way to go. It depends on how much cash you have left in your pocket. Tax rules regarding various kinds of invest-ments can make the difference between retiring comfortably, and not being able to retire at all. Highly taxed interest-bearing investments, coupled with inflation, could, slowly but surely, make you go backwards by eroding your savings over time.

Legitimate Ways to Beat the Taxman

Tax Deferrals
Tax deferrals are investments on which taxation is "deferred" or put off until a future date when you will be in a lower tax bracket.

Registered Retirement Savings Plans—RRSP
Once again, we stress the absolute importance of taking full advantage of RRSPs, once your home is well on the way to being paid off.

Registered Pension Plans—RPP
Chances are you're working for a company that has a registered pension plan for employees. To ensure you will have some income after you retire, your employer contributes an annual amount on your behalf to a registered pension plan. Employees may be permitted, or even required, to make additional contri-butions to the plan. But your annual contribution is a tax deduction. Once you retire, your pension income is taxed as you receive it on an annual basis.

Deferred Profit Sharing Plans—DPSP

Many companies offer, as a benefit, a "deferred profit sharing plan." They operate in the same way as a registered pension plan, in that contributions are made by the employer. Employer contributions to DPSPs, however, are based on profits rather than a fixed dollar amount each year per employee.

The tax advantage is similar to your pension plan. You aren't taxed on money put into your deferred profit sharing plan until you withdraw it, normally at retirement.

Such plans are normally used by smaller companies that do not wish to commit themselves to large pension contributions in case they end up losing money that year. DPSPs can also serve as incentives for greater employee productivity because they are based on profits.

Employer contribution limits for DPSPs increased in 1991 as part of the new pension reform legislation. Employee contributions to DPSPs are currently not permitted.

Housing

The profit made on the sale of the house you live in is not taxable. A handyman willing to move and make house repairs on a new home can consequently build up considerable home equity without being taxed.

Rental properties

Much if not all of the income earned from a rental property can be tax-free, because almost any expense involved in the operation of your rental property is tax-deductible. Advertising, repairs, maintenance, depreciation of appliances, home improvement, the interest portion of mortgage payments ... they can all be used as deductions against the rental payment.

If the allowable expenses offset the rental income, the taxman cannot charge you tax on that rental income. If you've bought a sound rental property, and made a large enough initial cash downpayment, then the rent should cover the cost of the mortgage and taxes.

One tip: The tax-deductible interest portion of the mortgage begins to dramatically dip as the mortgage goes down. It might make financial sense—once tax-breaks are figured into your equation—to remortgage a rental property and use the cash to either enhance the property (and hence its value) or place a down payment on another property. Keep the investment cycle alive!

Incorporation

Incorporation means placing a barrier between your personal assets and those of the company. If an incorporated business goes broke, then creditors cannot come after your personal assets.

The expenses of incorporating and filing business income-tax forms every year often outweigh the advantages—until such time as your side business is moving into the $40 000 to $50 000 a year gross income range.

Consult carefully with your accountant before considering incorporation.

Side businesses

Consulting, cleaning, summer gardening, pie-making, tele-marketing—there are literally hundreds of small businesses that can be run as a sideline out of your house.

If you are running a home business, then you can deduct the office space in your home, travel associated with the work, car expenses, entertaining of clients, part of your utility bills, and part of your property taxes.

With your own business, you can hire your spouse or family members as vice-presidents, treasurers, book-keepers. They can be paid a reasonable salary from the company. It's another way of splitting income with family earners who are in a lower tax bracket (see Income Splitting, below).

Farms can also be purchased as loss-leader side-line busi-nesses. But if you can afford to buy a farm as a tax write-off, you've moved beyond this introduction to saving money the old-fashioned way.

Income Splitting

Income splitting is a nifty concept accepted by the taxman. Your income can be split, for tax purposes, among members of your family. It's the old idea—three different incomes pay a lot less tax altogether, in lower tax brackets, than does one big income.

Spousal RRSP

If you are the top income-earner in your family, then you can contribute money to your wife or husband's RRSP. Yet you can still claim that deduction for yourself. For instance, if neither you nor your spouse has a pension plan, you can both put the individual maximum of $11 500 each into either person's RRSP.

After three years, your spouse can pull your contribution out of his or her RRSP, and have it taxed in his or her name.

Suppose you are both working. You stash funds in your wife's RRSP. Three years later, with a couple of small kids, your wife decides to stop working full-time. She can then pull that money out of her RRSP, and have it taxed at a much lower rate than you would have to pay. This makes dollars that are taxed at a lower rate available to your family much earlier than retirement time.

Spousal RRSPs work well within a stable family environment, where both partners are in financial harmony.

Like all these options, spousal RRSPs should be thoroughly reviewed with your accountant. The rules change from year to year. Our purpose is to alert you to these possibilities, and explain the basic concepts.

Registered Education Savings Plans—RESP

RESPs are income-splitting with your children, a recent innovation by the federal government that is still being tinkered with. In 1993, up to $31 500 in total (the amount is adjusted annually) could be deposited in a registered fund for each child's post-secondary education.

The dollars you invest (to a maximum of $1500 per year) cannot be declared as a tax deduction for yourself. But any income the fund earns from its investments is not taxed until withdrawn from the plan for educational purposes. When it is withdrawn, it is considered for tax purposes as part of your child's income.

Your child can withdraw money from a registered education savings plan, for educational purposes, while still in a low tax bracket. Money withdrawn from an education savings plan can be used for books, tuition fees, room and board, education travel, or field trips. And you can start an "RESP" for your child from the moment he or she is born.

If your child wants no formal education after high school, you or any other designated benefactor can withdraw money from the fund, as long as the money is used for higher learning. You could take flying lessons, or attend an institute that offers a round-the-world trip as part of its geography course. Because RESPs can be used for yourself, they can be useful financial planning tools. You can bank income for your child's education, or use that money for courses for yourself in a low income-tax year.

You also have the right to take your original cash out of the plan at any time, without restrictions on its use, and without paying further tax. If you invest $4000 in an RESP and then withdraw that $4000 seven years later, interest would still continue to build on the accumulated interest.

If none of your family or acquaintances wants to use the dollars in the education fund, the institution where the plan is registered gives the accrued interest over to an institute of higher learning. All you get back is your original investment.

In today's world, it's difficult to imagine any child who would not seek some form of further education where books, tuition fees, or educational travel are involved. RESPs make sense. Education will also become more and more expensive. Experts forecast that government will not keep subsidizing education at the generous levels of the 1970s and 1980s. An RESP may become a necessity to your child's educational aspirations.

The plan must be collapsed after 21 years.

Golden Rules for Avoiding the Taxman

1. Find a good, aggressive, creative accountant who charges reasonable rates. In 1993, a personal accountant could usually be hired for income tax purposes at $50 to $300, depending on how complex your return was.
2. It's your right to shelter all your income in as many ways as possible against income tax.
3. It can make the difference between a comfortable retirement and a financially limited one.
4. Consult the experts. See what you can do to keep your money for yourself, not for the government.

The Results of Non-Avoidance:
James Rollheiser

James Rollheiser ought to be well-off. At 48, he's making the best money of his life: $70 000 a year as an engineer for a medium-sized oil and gas engineering firm. Rollheiser's company was too small to have a company pension plan. And James didn't like the idea of RRSPs. He was convinced the government would change its mind, and suddenly tax the billions of dollars being held in Canadian RRSPs. He didn't believe in investing in anything risky. James wasn't interested in any investment that came with a tax break—rental homes, mutual funds, stocks, or any other tax shelters. All he purchased were Canada Savings Bonds. James' CSBs were earning 10%. But he lives in Quebec, where provincial and federal income taxes are over 50%. After taxes, the return on his CSBs was closer to 5% than 10%. With inflation running at 6% per year, James was in fact losing 1% of the value of his savings every year. When Rollheiser realized this he was angry. The whole system seemed against him. His friends at work were getting tax refunds of $2000 to $4000. But he'd wind up owing Revenue Canada an extra $6000 a year. He wasn't putting aside enough money for retirement. He thought the safest way was to leave his savings in the bank or in savings bonds, and let them grow. In fact, they were shrinking.

Post Retirement

Genius is nothing but a greater aptitude for patience.
                                    —Georges Lewis Leclerc Buffon
In this book we preach thrift, conservative values, and keeping
your hard-earned savings away from the taxman. There comes
a day, however, when Registered Retirement Savings Plans
(RRSPs) can no longer be used to defer taxes. Your RRSP is no
longer a valid tax shelter by your 71st birthday. If you haven't
made arrangements, your RRSP will suddenly be fair game for
the taxman. Without planning, a huge chunk of your long-
deferred RRSP income could disappear into the government's
general revenues.

Fortunately, there are ways you can continue to enjoy the
benefits of your hard-earned RRSP without having to take it all
out and pay tax on it when you hit the magic age of 71. In your
planning, remember you will probably be making staged with-
drawals from your RRSP well before you hit 71, especially if
you have opted for early retirement. The trick, as we've

discussed in earlier chapters, is withdrawing money from your RRSP in years when other income is low. For most people this occurs when they retire and they no longer can draw on a regular salary. The lower your total income for any given year, the less income tax you will have to pay.

Determining how much of your retirement nest egg you should spend each year is very much an individual decision. It's based on you and your spouse's health, your original nest egg, the lifestyle you want to lead, and economic factors beyond your control, like inflation.

With proper planning, you should have sufficient monthly income to enjoy yourself fully while you're healthy. If failing health forces you to slow down, then you still need enough financial resources to be comfortable.

Registered Retirement Income Funds—RRIFs

Although a registered retirement income fund can be opened at any age, it is primarily designed for the post-retiree to roll his or her RRSP money into, after RRSPs are collapsed at the age of 71.

Like RRSPs, there are basically two types of RRIFs: self-directed and conventional. In both types, your money is not taxed until it is withdrawn from the plan.

Self-directed RRIFs allow you to invest in the same wide variety of securities as the self-directed RRSP (see Chapter 3 for a complete list).

Conventional RRIFs usually invest in GICs or mutual funds, and someone else makes the investment decisions for you.

RRIFs differ from RRSPs in a number of ways.

With an RRIF, according to a taxation department formula, you *must* withdraw a certain amount of money every year from the plan. The formula is designed so that larger and larger chunks of the remaining capital in the fund are withdrawn year by year. There is a minimum amount you must withdraw from a RRIF every year (a formula based on age) but no maximum limit. You can take out as much as you want (as long as you are prepared to pay the income tax) and that amount can vary from year to year.

You are not allowed to put "new" capital into an RRIF. All funds going into a RRIF in the first place must come from collapsed RRSPs, or transfers from other RRIF's.

RRIFs are an increasingly attractive post-retirement investment vehicle, because with the new legislation they can continue for as long as you are alive. They provide a predictable monthly, quarterly, semi-annual, or annual source of income. By the nature of the formula, they slowly "bleed down" your investment. The actual value of the RRIF slowly declines as you move into your "old" old age.

At death, the RRIF goes to your beneficiary or your estate.

Annuities

Before RRIFs were introduced, annuities were really the only alternative for retirees not wanting to collapse their RRSPs and then pay taxes on them. The retiree gives an insurance or trust company a chunk of money. It can come from savings, a pension, or an RRSP rollover. In return, the financial institution promises you a set monthly income (the annuity) for either a fixed term or for the rest of your life.

A fixed term annuity usually expires when you and/or your spouse reach 90. A straight life annuity guarantees you and/or your spouse a predetermined monthly payment for the rest of your life.

Annuities come in a variety of shapes and forms, with various survivor packages. In all cases, however, the institution is investing your money on your behalf, giving you payments based on the growth of the investments, minus its own fee.

Annuities and RRIFs: Pros and Cons

Annuities are a worry-free retirement income package. You turn the investment decisions over to an institution, which guarantees its contract as long as the institution stays in business. Say, for instance, you had an annuity worth $100 000 which promised to pay you an 8.5% return. You'd receive $8500 a year, or a guaranteed monthly cheque of $780 until you or the term expired.

Like RRSPs and RRIFs, money in an annuity is tax-sheltered. You only pay tax on the amount that is taken out of the plan each year.

An RRIF gives you, as a conservative investor, much more flexibility than an annuity. You can change investments, pay-out schedules, et cetera. The capital is always yours. It will be passed on to your family or estate when you die and will not be absorbed by the financial institution—as happens with an annuity.

Over the long haul, it's likely an RRIF will earn a higher rate of return than an annuity. If you are a wise and experienced investor, you can profit from your own investment decisions. But, with an RRIF, nobody can stop you from investing poorly. There is always a chance you could lose your capital.

Pension Plans

Pension plans come in two basic packages—money purchase and defined benefit.

In a money purchase plan, your future retirement income is entirely based on the earnings of funds that go into the plan.

In the more popular defined benefit plan, you know from the beginning how much your pension will be when you retire. It's based on a percentage of your annual salary over a specified number of years. The pension fund manager is charged with ensuring the plan will be well enough funded in the future to meet your predetermined pension income. Your employer is also expected to contribute enough money to keep the plan solvent.

In cases where the employee is allowed to put money into the plan, it can act like forced savings. The money is deducted from your pay cheque before you can even get your hands on it.

Pension plans are not necessarily the perfect retirement vehicle. A number of pensions, including those of Alberta government employees, are dramatically underfunded. Because the employer has failed to put enough money into the fund, payments may not be as much as promised.

Tuning Up for Retirement:
Penny Polanski

Penny Polanski sold pianos all her life.

Penny is 75 now, and she and her husband have a retirement income of $65 000 a year.

Penny didn't do much out of the ordinary. She paid off her home as soon as possible. She made major contributions to her RRSP every year. Once her mortgage was paid off, she began to buy blue-chip stocks every year and reinvested all dividends. Being the kind of woman who liked to work, Polanski didn't retire until she was 72. She rolled $400 000 into National Housing Association mortgages—an investment that pays her $40 000 a year. The $200 000 she had in blue-chip stocks she left alone. After all, she was picking up about $14 000 a year in dividends. From the government's Canada Pension Plan, and from a small service pension, she picks up $11 000. Penny has no financial worries. She bird watches, goes fly fishing, works in her garden—and there's not a piano to be seen in her home.

Planning Your Family's Financial Future

Distrust and caution are the parents of security.
—Benjamin Franklin

For your family's sake, you need to insure your life, the lives of your family members, your assets, and your ability to work.

Life Insurance

If you have a family, there are some simple facts you must consider. The less wealth you have, the more life insurance you need. The more dependents you have, the more dependent you are on life insurance. As you get older and richer, you don't need as much life insurance as you did in earlier days.

Insurance is a simple proposition. You pay an insurance company a monthly premium based on dozens of factors. Should you die unexpectedly (and not by your own hand) your "designated beneficiaries" receive the total amount of insurance you have contracted for with the company.

Life insurance is a necessity. When you die, you want to leave your family with enough money to continue with the same lifestyle they now enjoy.

Most people purchase "term" life insurance. You are insured for a certain number of years, until the term expires. As you get older, the cost of such insurance rises. For estate-building, term insurance gives the best value. A rule of thumb is to insure yourself for ten times your annual salary.

Established businesses usually offer employees a basic life insurance plan that's less expensive than individual insurance. Often there's optional higher coverage available at reasonable rates.

"Whole life" insurance is still popular. You contribute to a combined life insurance and savings plan. When you reach the end of the term, you are no longer insured, but you do have a pay-out, a "cash-surrender" for the savings portion of the plan. However, whole life insurance is a poor investment. If you took the cost difference between term and whole life insurance, and placed it in something as safe as government bonds, then you would likely earn a better rate of return than most whole life plans.

Life insurance is ironic. You have to pay higher monthly premiums at a time of your life when you have high demands on your pay cheque. As you get older and wealthier, as the demands on your income drop and your savings grow, you don't have to spend as much on life insurance. You will have enough assets to be "self-insured." When you die, your family should be left with enough capital to live comfortably for the rest of their days.

Life insurance in all its forms must be periodically reviewed. Never forget to update all your insurance—up or down— depending on where you are in your long-term financial plan.

Mortgage Insurance

If you have a large mortgage on your home, then it makes sense to either insure your mortgage (if you die, the insurance auto- matically pays off the balance remaining) or take out more life insurance. As the mortgage goes down, the need for mortgage insurance diminishes.

Disability Insurance

The most neglected form of insurance is probably the most important. Your ability to work is an awfully big asset, yet statistics show your chances of being disabled are much higher, during any stage of your life, than premature death. If you can't work, disability insurance protects at least a portion of your current income. (You cannot be insured for 100% of your salary. Insurance companies only offer disability insurance based on 60% to 70% of your income.)

Insuring Your Assets

All your possessions should be insured against fire, damage, theft, and personal liability (your dog bites the mail carrier and she sues for $1 million). Make sure your coverage is on a par with the value of your possessions.

Wills

"I, J. Doe, of sound mind, do hereby leave all my hundreds of thousands to Fanatics For Fun, and the grandfather clock in the living room to my remaining son ..."

Write a will, if you have any assets at all. A will is nothing more than a plan to pass on your wealth in an orderly fashion. It can often be preventive medicine, a way to make sure the family doesn't fall apart after your death because of bitter infighting over the division of your assets.

Too many estates have ended up being spent on legal fees, as various claimants went to court to fight over the assets of people who left no wills.

A will can be as informal as a handwritten note. A standard will form can be purchased at a stationery store. It makes more sense, however, to spend a small amount to have your will correctly drawn up by a lawyer.

With a small estate, the "executor," the person responsible for tidying up your earthly affairs, can be your spouse or any responsible friend.

As your assets grow in size and complexity, the executor should be somebody with financial training, be it a friend or a professional executor working for a trust company. If your relationships are complicated (several marriages, step-children, acrimonious or contested divorce proceedings) the better off you are with an experienced executor.

A basic will should identify yourself, the person writing the will; revoke past wills; leave instructions for the winding up of your immediate financial affairs; identify the beneficiaries and what assets they are to receive; and stipulate where any left-over assets, after the beneficiaries are taken care of, should go.

If your children are still minors, it's a wise idea to name guardians in your will, in case you and your spouse die at the same time. Ensure there is a financial formula—worked out with your executor—that provides some compensation for the guardian, and for the children's expenses as they grow up. Consider a remarriage clause in each other's wills, and leave set amounts for each child.

In a worst-case scenario, you as a widowed spouse might be hoodwinked into another marriage by a shyster whose main aim is to spend your money. At least the shyster cannot get his or her greedy hands on money left directly for your children.

A will may seem like a needless exercise, especially if you are still young. But if you have no will, then your spouse does not automatically inherit all your property. Other relatives or business associates may file claims on the estate. The entire mess would have to go to court, taking years to settle. Without a will, you lose the right to appoint your own executor, and your spouse loses the right to divide the assets among your children. An estate left without a will is dispensed by a provincially-appointed executor in predetermined slices according to provincial statute. In effect, you are turning responsibility for the disposal of your assets to somebody whose ideas may be very different from your own. Because your no-will estate is bound by provincial regulations, your children cannot receive any of their inheritance until they reach a certain age specified by provincial legislation.

Taxes and Estate Planning

Rest assured, taxes on your assets will outlive you. As assets are sold, government collects tax. But some assets, your RRSP, your principal residence, and a family farm, can be passed to your spouse without immediate taxation. Money rolled from the deceased spouse's RRSP or RRIF into the survivor's RRSP or RRIF is not taxed. Your principal property, transferred to your spouse, isn't taxed until it is sold.

Estate Freezing

You can pass on the growth in your assets to your children while you are still alive, offering the great advantage of having that income taxed at much lower rates for them than if the money came into your now-wealthy hands.

You set up a company in which you and your children are the shareholders. Your shares are fixed in value, but your children's shares are free to grow. If your children sell their shares, they'll pay taxes in their income bracket, which is usually much lower than yours.

Family trusts and estate freezes are very complicated. They shouldn't be attempted without the help of a lawyer.

Why Bother with Insurance?:
Joe Slotek

Farmer Joe Slotek never bothered much with insurance. He took out a policy 15 years ago, but he'd never thought to update it. One day, Joe brought home a puppy. He put it in the barn next to his house. The poor little thing was cold, and so Joe hung a heat lamp for it. Darned if the little dog didn't chew right through the heat lamp cord. The short circuit set some straw on fire, the straw spread to the wood, the barn burned down, his house burned down, his car was destroyed.

Joe took out his insurance policy. He was insured … for $20 000, when the value of what he had lost was over a quarter-million dollars. Joe was 62 when the fire happened—too old to start over. He bought an $8000 house trailer and a $3000 car. Now he's deciding what he should do next. The only good thing is that the dog got out of the fire, and is a faithful and loyal companion to this day.

Picking Your Financial Team

Chance favors the mind that's prepared.

—Louis Pasteur

Some lawyers, bankers, accountants, stockbrokers, and insurance agents have more interest in their interests than in your interests. The team, however, is vital. The banker gets your money, the accountant keeps your money away from the taxman, the lawyer takes care of those deals you cannot do on a handshake, the insurance agent protects you against disaster—and the broker helps you make money. You have to trust your team. You have to like, or at least respect, their abilities. Word-of-mouth reputation is all important. Check with friends who have the same conservative financial goals as you. Who do they use? Are your friends happy with the service provided? Don't be afraid to shop around. Try potential advisors out on smaller deals. See how they perform before you commit your life's savings.

Being on a first name basis with your banker is essential. If the bankers know you, and have had enough dealings with you to form an opinion of your credit-worthiness, getting loans is a far less stringent process. There comes a time when you need to borrow—for emergencies, for an RRSP, for that once-in-a-lifetime investment. That's when your banker can help.

The more investments you have, the more need you have for an accountant. Keeping the wealth you accumulate is absolutely dependent on your accountant. He or she should know all the rules of taxation. The fee is small compared to the tax savings he or she should find for you. Until you're a big investor, you don't need to go to an accounting firm where 30 cents of every dollar is spent on interior design and fancy presentations. It's just not necessary, and it will cost you more than an accountant who specializes in working with ordinary people.

Accounting is as much an art as a science. Because so much of taxation is based on interpretation and justification, you need an aggressive, creative accountant who knows what's happening inside the minds of the tax collectors from year to year.

A good accountant helps you with your planning. He's one of your main financial advisors. Ask around. Look for someone who's at a level close to yours, with the same financial outlook.

Lawyers aren't quite as necessary … until you *really* need them. Your lawyer shouldn't mind doing the small stuff—setting up your will, doing the legal work for your real estate, helping plan your estate for your kids. Don't be afraid to compare prices. Some lawyers are notorious for handing out huge bills that the client, because of inexperience, is hesitant to question.

Most insurance agents are salespeople on commission. Go to a reputable firm. Find an agent who's willing to shop around on your behalf to find the best deals for the protection you want on your home, life, and automobile. (Often the best life insurance plan can be purchased through the company you work for.)

Some stockbrokers are of the "churn-and-burn" school, and can be a little too greedy for their own good. They don't make much money from the long-term appreciation of your assets. They make money from the commissions they earn on encouraging you to buy and sell. These stockbrokers are pretty easy to spot. Despite your carefully explained financial pyramid and your need for long-term investments, they will always recommend you buy this, or sell that. On the other hand, a good stockbroker in a "full-service" firm can provide you with every investment opportunity described in this book, with the exception of real estate. If they are reputable, listen carefully to your needs, and provide sound conservative advice, they should be able to find you good reliable investment vehicles.

Find a conservative broker through the recommendations of friends you trust. Or phone the firm, and ask the manager to recommend an individual in the office who suits your investment profile. Divide up your portfolio between two brokers for a couple of years. See which one you like the best.

The reputation of your financial advisors is all important. Thoroughly check the credibility of your potential team before entrusting them with your future security.

Ten Ways to Blow Your Investment

There's a sucker born every minute.

—P.T. Barnum

1. Letting Greed Cloud Reason

Why do we all fall prey to greed? Why do most people—sane, reasonable, middle-class people—think it's possible to find an investment that will multiply 100 times within 10 minutes of making that investment?

This book reminds you that there's no magic formula for getting rich. But greed seems to be a basic of human nature. We ignore the symptoms—the stock promoter who claims the once-in-a-lifetime deal is a "limited opportunity" with a "limited time offer."

Greed is the buoyant optimism that comes with profit. If the stock's gone up 30%, why not 200%! Wisdom tells you it's time to sell. Greed makes you hang on, thinking you'll make a million.

Sell when you've made a reasonable profit. The herd—that's the stockbrokers' favourite term for group mentality—never realizes when the party is over.

2. Letting Fear Paralyse Reason

Fear is the greatest impediment to making money. Fear creates the herd mentality. When a stock is low, there is fear it will be lower, and a general stampede to sell sets in. The herd does not realize when a good stock is a bargain. The herd doesn't realize how sensible it is to buy more of a good stock, when its fortunes are at an ebb. For it will likely soar again.

Gold is a classic example of fear paralysing reason. When gold was selling at record-high levels of $850 an ounce, people lined up outside gold-selling institutions across Canada to buy more. But, when gold was selling for $280 an ounce, nobody could be found to buy an ounce.

Herd mentality has been with society since the Neanderthals. The intelligent loner, who pulls away from the stampede of panic, who doesn't take the popular press or fearful friends too seriously, usually makes the bucks. Most small investors, driven by greed and fear, miss the party. It's over when they arrive. Or they leave before it begins.

3. Insufficient Firepower

Firepower is the ability to ride out the storms, in order to bask in the sunshine of the good times. Firepower is proper planning: having enough cash on hand to meet all the requirements of day-to-day living, without having to cash in long-term investments prematurely because of an emergency. An example: Your broker offers you an excellent stock that has fallen from $27 to $16. It's a good deal, because the company is expected to bounce back in the short- to medium-term. You scoop up every dime, every loonie, to buy a stock you know will let you retire ten years ahead of schedule. Two months later, the orthodontist is pounding on the door. The kids' teeth will cost $3000. But your money is all tied up. The stock you're so sure about has continued on a minor slide to $13. You don't have the "firepower" to ride the recovery to $25 in two years' time. You unload the stock, the most liquid asset you have, for $13. Murphy's Law: The need to fix the family teeth will always occur when your investments are at their lowest ebb.

The conservative investor always keeps a cushion of financial reserves—bonds, savings, whatever is highly liquid and not depreciable. Hold on to your long-term investments through lean times.

4. Abandoning Your Financial Plan

Nothing can be more disastrous than losing sight of your own financial goals. Every investment dangled before your nose must be considered within the overall context of your financial plan. Remember your financial pyramid, with a large base of conservative investments and a small tip of speculative ones. Where does the investment fit in? Can you afford a high-risk, high-reward proposition without upsetting the balance of your pyramid? If you abandon your plan, then you are an obvious target for those two horsemen of the financial apocalypse, Fear and Greed. Good brokers will tell you, in a moment of truth, that they've never had a wealthy client who didn't stick to a financial game plan.

5. Being Seduced by the "Rich" Stereotype

We've all seen the flashy television "documentaries" on the incredible entrepreneur who has made millions by putting everything on the line, on every venture, and always comes out on the winning end. They get all the media attention. But the fact is the "high roller" is but 1 out of 10 000 wealthy individuals. The other 9999 made their money the quiet, old-fashioned, careful way.

There is this quaint notion that wealth is to be flaunted. Owning a Mercedes-Benz, a huge house with a swimming pool, and having a dozen credit cards in your wallet must mean you have cash to burn. Hah! As we've said before, most wealthy individuals are low-key folks. Those who are the most image-conscious usually haven't accumulated wealth. It's the line of credit, and the accumulated savings that count … not the colour of the credit card.

6. Mistaking Extravagance for Comfort

Making money the old-fashioned way calls for a small measure of discipline. You learn to enjoy yourself without being indulgent. The money saved will make you wealthy by the time you retire. What's the big deal about owning an $80 000 car, when a

$10 000 vehicle will still get you to the same place in the same time in the same comfortable fashion? Does a person really need a 4000 or 8000 square-foot house, when 2000 square feet is most comfortable for an average family? Who can tell the difference between a well-made $400 suit and a $1200 suit that status-conscious men seek out?

Of course you're thrifty! Enjoy your thrift! Take pride in your ability to spot bargains. There's no need to make tremendous sacrifices to lifestyle. A little deferred gratification will do.

7. The Know-It Alls

Some people think they know it all. Highly specialized professionals can be the worst. Because they are most knowledgeable about certain areas, they assume they know about all things. But if you think you know everything, it's amazing how fast you'll find out how little you know—usually at the expense of your pocketbook. Be humble. Admit you don't know absolutely everything, and ask others for advice. It's surprising how much important information is available free of charge.

8. Under-Diversification

In this department, the honours go to some people dealing in real estate. They continue to insist, through busts and booms, that they can't go wrong in real estate. They don't start RRSPs, have no savings accounts, no stocks—they put all their money into real estate, with a minimum down payment. They "know" real estate will go up. In the great Alberta Crash of 1980-82, however, many realtors went from millionaire to pauper status.

There is the argument that you should stick to investing in the field you know best. There's an equally compelling argument to diversify, to spread your investments around so that you won't be knocked out by one company failure, or a recession in one particular sector of the economy, or a recession in one region. When the Principal Group collapsed in Western Canada in the late 1980s, thousands of Canadians were left financially strapped for years. They put all their investment eggs into what they had thought was a secure basket.

9. Impatience

Patience is the key to gradual financial success. Be patient while real estate temporarily dips in value, while stocks decline, while your city's economy goes through a cycle of hard times. Building your investments is a long, slow, sometimes boring process. Work on your overview. There's the need to detach yourself from the guaranteed-rate-of-return mentality. Stocks and mutual funds are not going to grow at a steady 10% per year. They may drop in value for a year or two. And then, in ten years, they may triple.

If you expect to see a fixed, guaranteed increase on your assets every month, accept that aspect of your own financial nature, and invest exclusively in GICs and fail-safe bonds. You will feel better. You'll forsake the historic fact that the stock market has consistently earned a few percentage points more than those guaranteed investments, but you'll have peace of mind.

Patience is crucial. The pay-offs will come after a long period of watching your investments grow.

10. Stagnation

There are plans, and there are plans. It's better to be obstinate, stubborn, and unbending about your financial plan than to have no plan at all. But if your financial plan grows with you, if it gradually changes its shape and investment strategy over the years, then you'll do better than those who haven't changed their strategy since 1956.

We are not advising complete turn-abouts, but steady evolution. Investment strategies in the 1970s were predicated on high inflation. Those same investments, like gold and oil, have not done as well in the relatively slow inflation of the 1980s and early 1990s.

Those who were convinced interest rates would jump back up to 18% insisted on keeping their ready cash in 4% savings accounts. They were waiting for the day they could invest in bonds during inflationary times. They kept waiting, while the average interest rate dropped to less than 8% in the mid-1980s.

Make small changes in your plan as you go. Give yourself 5% – 10% "play" on each level of your pyramid. Nothing is written in stone in the business world. Most financial plans have options and fluidity. There are always several different routes to successful conservative investing.

Expanding Your Financial Education

*My years in Wall Street and business became
one long course of education in human nature.*

—Bernard Baruch

If you want to be a top-notch investor, you can never stop learning. Continuing education courses in investing are useful. They're offered at most universities and community colleges. Stay in touch with business trends. Subscribe to one of Canada's three major business newspapers, *The Globe & Mail*, the *Financial Post*, or the *Financial Times*.

We recommend books that have stood the test of time.

Charles MacKay's *Extraordinary Popular Delusions and the Madness of Crowds* was first published over 200 years ago. A crowd psychology classic, it documents how investment psychology over the past 500 years has swung from greed to total despair. This is a "must read" for anyone looking for information on the psychology of investment.

Bernard Baruch is one of the most successful American investors ever. He was an advisor to presidents on both government and personal financial policy. His book *My Story*, written in the early 20th century, is one of the best for explaining how to think for yourself, and for analysing world events and trends to determine what areas of the economy will do well. Baruch writes in an informal, anecdotal manner that is a joy to read.

More contemporary is Peter Lynch's *One Up on Wall Street*. Lynch, one of the most successful money managers of our times, explains how he made his fortune buying and selling stocks.

The Intelligent Investor, by Ben Graham, is a perceptive guide to evaluation—how to recognize when there's good value in an investment. His book is especially useful in evaluating securities (stocks and bonds).

David Chilton has written a fascinating book called *The Wealthy Barber*. It is a fictional story about Roy the wealthy barber who gives out common-sense pearls of financial wisdom as he cuts peoples hair. This book is highly entertaining and perfect for those who find the topic of financial planning dull or intimidating.

Retiring Wealthy is written by Gordon Pape. This is one of the few financial books that is geared to the Canadian perspective. The book offers a comprehensive, step by step approach to setting and then meeting financial goals. It is considered a "must-read" for any Canadian who wants to retire with financial security.

If you wish to specialize in the buying and selling of stocks, three investment newsletters stand out from the hundreds of tip-sheets available. They cost between $100 and $300 a year per subscription, and are also available in major public libraries.

Zweig Forecast has been the number one ranked U.S. research report over the last 10 years.

The Investment Reporter has performed the same feat among Canadian investment newsletters.

Investment Quality Trends focuses on blue-chip, dividend-paying stocks, and is therefore ideal for the old-fashioned conservative investor. In addition, the newsletter has earned itself a sterling "investment pick" reputation. The investments it has suggested have averaged 20% growth per year over the past 10 years.

Conclusion

If one tells the truth, one is sure, sooner or later, to be found out.
— Oscar Wilde

There's one lesson you should now know: creating wealth the old-fashioned way doesn't take a tremendous amount of brains or risk. The old-fashioned way is simplicity itself—setting up realistic goals, and, over the long-term, getting a little closer to those goals day by day.

The combination of good planning, common-sense investing, and long-term compounding is unbeatable. Any hardworking, practical individual should be able to achieve enough financial wealth to be able to retire comfortably—with any luck, a little ahead of schedule. It doesn't matter if you're a cabbie, a sales clerk, or a highly paid professional. You will eventually achieve a comfortable financial position by following the principles in this book.

Investing the old-fashioned way works. Why not let it work for you?

Glossary

Accountant: A person who organizes financial information

Accrued interest: The accumulated interest on a loan

Amortization: The time period over which payments on a loan are made

Amortization period: The time period it takes before a loan is completely repaid

Annuity: An investment that returns your principal and interest in a series of regular payments

Assets: The things you own

Back-end loaded mutual fund: A mutual fund where the sales commission is paid at the time of selling

Bear market: A stock market where the average share price is declining

Blue-chip stock: Shares issued by large, well-financed, profitable, and established companies

Bonds: IOUs with a set interest rate, backed by collateral, issued by governments and corporations and repaid over a fixed period. (*See* debenture.)

Bull market: A stock market where the average share price is rising

Call option: A speculative investment, in effect a bet, that a stock, bond, or other financial vehicle will rise in value

Canada Savings Bond (CSB): A bond sold to the public by the Government of Canada every October, with units as small as $100

Capital gains: Profit from the sale of an asset

Closed mortgage: A mortgage with restrictions on the accelerated pay-down of the principal

Closed-end mutual fund: A mutual fund where the units are bought and sold on the open market

Collateral: Assets promised by a borrower to a lender in case a loan cannot be paid back

Commodity fund: A mutual fund that invests in commodities

Common share: Basic unit of ownership in a company

Company: An entity created for the purpose of carrying on a business

Compound interest: The process of adding interest payments on to the original loaned amount as the payments come due, thereby creating a larger loan amount on which more interest can be earned

Convertible bond/debenture: A bond or debenture that can be exchanged for shares in a company

Convertible preferred shares: Dividend-paying shares that can also be exchanged for common shares at a predetermined price within a specified length of time

Coupon: The detachable part of a bond entitling the holder to a cash payment of the interest owing on a specific date

Currency: The money used by any nation

Debenture: A bond not backed with collateral. (*See* bond.)

Deferred profit-sharing plan (DPSP): A plan where a portion of a company's profits is put into savings and investments to benefit employees

Defined benefit pension plan: A pension where the amount to be paid out is spelled out in advance

Depreciation: The drop in value of an asset due to age

Disability insurance: Purchased insurance that pays you in case you become unemployed due to disability

Dividend: Cash paid on a regular basis to the owner of a stock by the company

Dividend-income fund: A mutual fund where most of the investments are purchased because of the dividends they produce

Dollar-cost averaging: Averaging out the cost of purchasing units of an investment (e.g. stocks) by buying fixed amounts of the investment on a regular basis over a number of years

Earned income: A technical term used by Revenue Canada to describe earnings from employment minus certain deductions

Equity: Ownership position in a large asset, usually expressed in a percentage relationship between the owner's investment and the amount borrowed to complete the purchase

Estate: Assets left behind upon death

Estate freezing: For taxation purposes, a method of transferring assets to one's heirs before death

Estate planning: Planning for the dispersal of assets once the asset-holder has died

Executor: In the case of a will, the person or institution named to carry out the instructions in a will

Extendable bond/debenture: The right of the issuer to extend the date of maturity on a bond or debenture by a specified number of years

Fixed income investment: Investment that offers a fixed, regular return

Fixed interest rate: A predetermined interest rate that will not change over the duration of the loan

Floating-rate preferred shares: Preferred shares where the dividend rate moves up and down in relation to the prime rate (the interest rate banks charge to their best customers)

Front-end loaded mutual fund: A mutual fund where the sales commission is paid at the time of purchase

Futures: A contract to buy or sell a commodity at a fixed price at a future date

Gold bullion: Large quantities of gold, usually in bar form

Growth stock: A stock where added value is expected to come from a much higher share price in the future

Guaranteed investment certificate (GIC): A certificate issued by banks or trust companies that guarantees a set rate of return on an investment over a fixed period

Income fund: A mutual fund that purchases high-yield, low-risk investments

Income splitting: Splitting of one person's income with two or more people, usually for taxation purposes

Incorporation: The establishment of a business as a legal entity

Inflation: The annual increase in the cost of living

Insurance: Purchased financial protection, usually on a yearly premium basis, against various kinds of loss or risk

Interest: The "rent" paid on borrowed money

Interest rate: The agreed upon amount of "rent" to be paid for borrowing money

Investment portfolio: The collection of various kinds of investments held by an individual or a corporation

Junior stock: Stock issued by young, start-up companies

Junk bond: A high-risk, high-interest bond issued by a company usually in poor financial condition

Leverage: The borrowing of money to buy something. The more money borrowed (compared to the amount of cash), the more "leveraged" the investment.

Liabilities: Money owed to someone else

Life insurance: Purchased financial protection for one's dependents upon one's death

Long-term return: Return on an investment over a long time

Maturity: The date when money loaned or borrowed for an investment has to be paid back in full, with interest

Money market fund: A mutual fund that purchases government and corporation interest-bearing investments, generally maturing in under one year

Money purchase pension plan: A pension plan based on the growth of the plan's investments, with no guarantee as to the amount paid out at retirement

Mortgage: Money borrowed from a financial institution to buy property

Mutual fund: A professionally managed company that invests large pools of capital on behalf of smaller investors

Net worth: The value of things you own, minus the money you owe

No-load mutual fund: A mutual fund where no fee is charged on the buying or selling of its units

Numismatic value: The worth of a coin based on what a collector will pay to buy it

Open mortgage: A mortgage that has no restrictions on the accelerated pay-down of the principal

Open-ended mutual fund: A mutual fund that buys its units back directly from its investors

Option: A stock market "bet" that a particular investment will rise or fall in value over a short period of time

Option fund: A mutual fund that invests in options

Pay-down: Paying off a loan at a faster rate than is spelled out in the terms of the loan agreement, usually a mortgage

Penny stocks: Shares that are usually valued at less than $1

Pension plan: A savings plan intended to provide an income after retirement

Precious metal fund: A mutual fund that invests in precious metals

Precious metals: Metals mined for their monetary rather than their manufacturing value

Preferred share: A kind of share that pays an annual return, or dividend, and has priority over the common shareholder should the company go bankrupt

Principal: The actual amount of money owing on a mortgage or a loan, not including the interest

Private company: A company whose shares are not traded on a stock market

Promissory note: A written promise to repay borrowed money

Promoter: Someone who hopes to profit from promoting the virtues of an investment

Public company: A company whose shares are traded on a stock market

Put option: A speculative investment, a bet that a stock, bond, or other financial vehicle will quickly fall in value. (*See* options.)

Rate of return: The amount of profit to be made on an investment, usually expressed as a percentage of the original amount

Registered educational savings plans (RESP): A government-registered savings plan that, if used for the future post-secondary education of a child, offers some tax advantages

Registered pension plan: Government-registered plan where both the employer and employee contribute to the employee's retirement fund

Registered Retirement Income Fund (RRIF): Government-registered accounts with financial institutions, into which seniors can, subject to certain conditions, transfer RRSP funds. These transferred funds are not taxed until withdrawn from the plan.

Registered Retirement Savings Plan (RRSP or RSP): A government registered account with any financial institution that allows money to be set aside and not taxed until it's withdrawn from the account, usually upon retirement

Retractable bond/debenture: A bond or debenture where the purchaser has the option of cashing in the bond or debenture at a previously agreed-upon price and time

Rights: An investment that gives the holder the ability to buy a stock at a fixed price for a very short time, e.g., one month. Rights are usually offered to shareholders already holding stock in the company.

RSP: *See* Registered Retirement Savings Plan

Runaway inflation: When the cost of living dramatically increases each year

Shares: *See* stocks

Short-selling: A stock market trading technique that can create a profit from the drop in the price of a stock

Speculative investments: Investments that come with both a high risk of losing your money, and the possibility of earning a high rate of return

Stock: Certificates representing ownership in a company

Stock market: A financial marketplace where most types of investments can be bought and sold

Strip coupon: An interest coupon that is physically separated from a bond: it can be bought and sold as a separate investment and promises a certain return to maturity. Strip coupons can be bought and sold before they come due.

Sweat equity: The use of one's labour to enhance the value of an asset

Tax: Money collected by the government

Tax deferral: Paying taxes on money earned at a future date, rather than in the current calendar year

Taxable income: Income that Revenue Canada considers taxable

Taxation: The compulsory payment of money to a government

Term: A fixed period of time, usually in relationship to the payment of money

Term deposits: An investment that earns a fixed rate of return over a fixed time period

Term life insurance: Life insurance purchased for a certain number of years

Treasury Bills: A form of short-term borrowing by the federal government from institutional lenders

Variable interest rate: A loan where the interest rate fluctuates in accordance with market conditions

Warrant: The option to buy a stock at a fixed price over a set period of time, usually issued to "sweeten" the sale of new stock

Whole life insurance: A combined life insurance and savings plan

Will: A plan to pass on one's wealth in an orderly fashion after one's demise

Windfall profit: Profit that comes swiftly and unexpectedly

Index